THE GIFTS
OF
THE GODS

APULIA FELIX AMONG GREEKS
INDIGENOUS AND ROMANS

永恒的绚美

希腊时代彩陶及普利亚艺术文化特展

南京市博物总馆
中国文物交流中心
意大利普利亚博物馆联盟

编 著

Nanjing Museum Administration

Art Exhibitions China

Poli Biblio-Museali della Regione Puglia Italia

文物出版社

图书在版编目（CIP）数据

永恒的绚美：希腊时代彩陶及普利亚艺术文化特展 /
南京市博物总馆，中国文物交流中心，意大利普利亚博物
馆联盟编著 . -- 北京：文物出版社，2024.3
ISBN 978-7-5010-8330-5

Ⅰ. ①永… Ⅱ. ①南… ②中… ③意… Ⅲ. ①彩陶 –
陶器（考古）– 意大利 – 图集 Ⅳ. ① K885.466.32

中国国家版本馆 CIP 数据核字 (2023) 第 249852 号

永恒的绚美
希腊时代彩陶及普利亚艺术文化特展

THE GIFTS OF THE GODS
APULIA FELIX AMONG GREEKS, INDIGENOUS AND ROMANS

编　　著｜南京市博物总馆
　　　　　中国文物交流中心
　　　　　意大利普利亚博物馆联盟
主　　编｜谭　平　许　强
责任编辑｜吕　游
责任印制｜王　芳
装帧设计｜雅昌设计中心
出版发行｜文物出版社
社　　址｜北京市东城区东直门内北小街 2 号楼
邮　　编｜100007
网　　址｜http://www.wenwu.com
经　　销｜新华书店
印　　刷｜北京雅昌艺术印刷有限公司
开　　本｜889mm×1194mm　1/16
印　　张｜17.25
版　　次｜2024 年 3 月第 1 版
印　　次｜2024 年 3 月第 1 次印刷
书　　号｜ISBN 978-7-5010-8330-5
定　　价｜380.00 元

南京市博物总馆策展团队
THE CURATORIAL TEAM OF NANJING MUSEUM ADMINISTRATION

总策划｜许强

Chief planner｜Xu Qiang

总监制｜吴阗　曾军　张成英

Chief supervisors｜Wu Tian　Zeng Jun　Zhang Chengying

展览统筹｜宋燕

Exhibition coordinator｜Song Yan

展览策划｜张蕾

Curator｜Zhang Lei

协助策划｜经赟　朱晓雪

Assistant curators｜Jing Yun　Zhu Xiaoxue

展览宣传｜毛晓玲　吕晓萌　彭侃　沈梦之　杨晓慧　薛琛　胡亚春

Publicity coordinators｜Mao Xiaoling　Lü Xiaomeng　Peng Kan　Shen Mengzhi　Yang Xiaohui　Xue Chen　Hu Yachun

展览文创｜贺湘　韩巍　陆甜甜　张莹莹　李昕

Creative product coordinators｜He Xiang　Han Wei　Lu Tiantian　Zhang Yingying　Li Xin

教育活动｜李舟　周雨璟　顾子淳　陈东东　王道程　管锦绣　吴雨伦

Educational Activities｜Li Zhou　Zhou Yujing　Gu Zichun　Chen Dongdong　Wang Daocheng　Guan Jinxiu　Wu Yulun

项目协助｜郑滢　戴路　俞瑾　黄贵成　狄海宁　倪羽佳　田萌　史慧倩　王光明　石朗君　陶颖　萧雅帆　韩金璋　熊鹏　丁易

Project assistants｜Zheng Ying　Dai Lu　Yu Jin　Huang Guicheng　Di Haining　Ni Yujia　Tian Meng　Shi Huiqian　Wang Guangming　Shi Langjun　Tao Ying　Xiao Yafan　Han Jinzhang　Xiong Peng　Ding Yi

信息技术｜彭坚　陆德洛　杨春纯

Information technology support｜Peng Jian　Lu Deluo　Yang Chunchun

管理建议｜叶家宽　戴长栋

Management advisors｜Ye Jiakuan　Dai Changdong

展厅保障｜施保宁　李海波　王超　何俊仁　徐晓峰　汪玉　徐智　杨晓宇

Exhibition hall logistics support｜Shi Baoning　Li Haibo　Wang Chao　He junren　Xu Xiaofeng　Wang Yu　Xu Zhi　Yang Xiaoyu

讲解服务｜"六朝青"志愿服务社

Guide service｜Volunteer Service Team—The Oriental Metropolitan Museum(The 3rd-6th Century)

中国文物交流中心策展团队
CURATORIAL TEAM OF ART EXHIBITIONS CHINA

总策划｜谭平

Chief planner ｜ Tan Ping

总监制｜周宇

Chief supervisor ｜ Zhou Yu

展览策划｜罗利君

Curator ｜ Luo Lijun

执行策展｜王宇

Executive curator ｜ Wang Yu

统筹执行｜施王欢　王卓然

Coordinators ｜ Shi Wanghuan　Wang Zhuoran

展览实施｜张沁芳　马平

Implementers ｜ Zhang Qinfang　Ma Ping

意大利策展团队
ITALIAN ORGANIZING COMMITTEE

普利亚大区文化旅游与领土部（主策展人）｜安娜·露西娅·坦佩斯塔

Dipartimento Turismo, Economia della Cultura e Valorizzazione del Territorio Regione Puglia (coordinamento) ｜ Anna Lucia TEMPESTA

莱切图书馆博物馆中心｜亚历山德拉·贝尔塞利

Polo Bibliomuseale di Lecce ｜ Alessandra BERSELLI

巴里市考古、美术和景观监管局｜文森扎·迪斯塔西

Soprintendenza Archeologia, Belle Arti e Paesaggio per la Città Metropolitana di Bari ｜ Vincenza DISTASI

普利亚公共剧院 — 地区艺术和文化联盟｜桑特·利凡特

Teatro Pubblico Pugliese - Consorzio regionale per le Arti e la Cultura ｜ Sante LEVANTE

莱切图书馆博物馆中心｜马尔切拉·努佐

Polo Bibliomuseale di Lecce ｜ Marcella NUZZO

莱切图书馆博物馆中心｜巴塞尔·赛

Polo Bibliomuseale di Lecce ｜ Basel SAI

布林迪西图书馆博物馆中心｜丹尼尔·斯佩迪卡蒂

Polo Bibliomuseale di Brindisi ｜ Daniele SPEDICATI

中国巡展组织团队
CHINA ITINERANT EXHIBITION ORGANIZING COMMITTEE

深圳市普兰迪营销策划有限公司

SHENZHEN PLD MARKETING PLANNING Co.,LTD

中国巡展总负责、展览当代部分策展｜洪泉

General director of China Itinerant Exhibition（Contemporary Curatorial）｜Hong Quan

中国巡展国际沟通负责｜柯西莫·德尔·维奇奥

Responsible for International Communication of China Itinerant Exhibition｜Cosimo Del Vecchio

项目经理｜许明恒

Project manager｜Kevin Xu

资料设计（意大利资料设计）｜赵宇宁

Italian exhibition material design｜Zhao Yuning

展览设计制作团队
THE DESIGN AND PRODUCTION TEAM

金山河（南京）文化发展有限公司

Jinshanhe (Nanjing) Cultural Development Co. Ltd.

展陈设计｜张抗　吴宇光　杨晓男　施铃　杨诗源　王澳

Exhibition design｜Zhang Kang　Wu Yuguang　Yang Xiaonan　Shi Ling　Yang Shiyuan　Wang Ao

展览制作｜洪尊益　杨陵　周冬兰　张毅　姚维捷

Exhibition production｜Hong Zunyi　Yang Ling　Zhou Donglan　Zhang Yi　Yao Weijie

现场图片拍摄｜施东升

Photography of the site｜Shi Dongsheng

Civilizations thrive through diversity and communication, mutually influencing and evolving. From the romantic Mediterranean to the ancient capital of the Six Dynasties-- Nanjing, the ancient Greek and Chinese civilizations, though rooted in different regions, share a vibrant vitality and profound influence spanning centuries.

Embracing the beautiful vision of harmonious development among diverse civilizations, Nanjing Museum Administration, in collaboration with eight Italian museums facilitated by the Art Exhibitions China, presents this exhibition at its branch, the Oriental Metropolitan Museum (the 3rd-6th Century). This marks a significant endeavor by Nanjing Museum Administration to foster cultural exchange and mutual learning. The success of this exhibition underscores Nanjing Museum Administration's commitment to building a robust public cultural service system. It reflects the effectiveness of resource allocation based on the core public cultural service product—exhibitions—and aligning them with audience-oriented demands.

This exhibition injects vitality into the development of Sino-Italian cultural relations, serving as a bridge to promote mutual understanding between the two nations. Through meticulous artifact selection, detailed textual analysis, and creative exhibition design, over a hundred treasures of ancient Greek civilization are beautifully presented. Following the exhibition's launch, Nanjing Museum Administration's curatorial team has provided vivid interpretations through various media channels and accompanying activities. The exhibition's compelling presentation reflects the Chinese cultural sector's appreciative and respectful attitude toward different civilizations, showcasing its ability to fulfill cultural missions.

致 辞

南京市博物总馆馆长
许　强

As a comprehensive showcase of the exhibition's landscape, this catalog features exquisite artifacts on display, media promotional content, exhibition design drafts, and articles from Italian archaeologists. On this occasion, I extend heartfelt thanks on behalf of Nanjing Museum Administration to the dedicated personnel from both China and Italy, whose efforts have contributed to the successful realization of the exhibition and catalog. In the future, Nanjing Museum Administration will seize this exhibition as an opportunity, continuing to act as a cultural link, unveiling innovative and distinctive exhibitions. This approach aims to allow visitors not only to understand the exhibition and its stories but also to continuously absorb the nourishment and wisdom of different civilizations, enhancing cultural identity and fostering cultural confidence.

文明因多样而交流，因交流而互鉴，因互鉴而发展。从浪漫的地中海到"六朝"古都南京，古希腊文明和华夏文明虽生发于不同的地域，却有着一样绵延千年的蓬勃生机和深远的影响力。

秉承多样文明和谐发展的美好愿景，南京市博物总馆通过中国文物交流中心引进，与意大利八家博物馆合作，在总馆分支机构六朝博物馆落地实施本次展览，这是南京市博物总馆促进文化交流与文明互鉴的一次重要实践。展览的成功举办，是南京市博物总馆重视公共文化服务体系建设、探索核心公共文化服务产品资源配置以及观众需求导向的成效体现。

此次展览的举办为中意文化关系的发展注入了活力，在促进两国民心相通方面发挥了桥梁作用。参与展览各环节筹备工作的中外工作人员严格遴选文物、细致梳理文本，通过巧妙的设计布陈，将百余件古希腊文明遗珍完美呈现。展览的策划是各方策展团队实现相互理解、相互认同的过程。展览开展后，总馆策展团队通过多种渠道的媒体宣传及配套活动组织，对展览进行不间断地生动诠释。展览所呈现的动人面貌，体现了中国文博界对于不同文明欣赏、尊重的认知态度，以及担当文化使命的能力水平。

作为展览景观的全貌展示，本图册收录了精美的展出文物，以及媒体宣传文字、展陈形式设计图稿与意大利考古学家的文章。值此付梓之际，我谨代表南京市博物总馆，向为展览付出辛劳，并促成展览和图册最终完美呈现的中意两国工作人员致以衷心谢忱。今后，南京市博物总馆将以此次展览为契机，继续发挥文化纽带作用，不断推出特色创新展陈，让公众在参观了解展览及其背后故事的同时，汲取不同文明的营养和智慧，增进文化认同，坚定文化自信。

China and Italy are outstanding examples representing eastern and western civilizations respectively. From the ancient Silk Roads to Marco Polo's journey around China to the Chinese classics "Four Books" translated by Italian missionary Matteo Ricci, the two great civilizations have interacted across thousands of miles, appreciating and influencing each other over some 2,000 years. Since the 1990s, cultural heritage institutions and museums in China and Italy have seen ever-increasing exchange of exhibitions and, in particular, their collaborations have continued to deepen in past several years. A great variety of exhibitions on Italian artifacts and artworks presented by Art Exhibitions China have attracted numerous Chinese viewers, enriching their spiritual and cultural lives.

Desirous of pushing China-Italy cultural exchanges and cooperation to a new height, Art Exhibitions China and Nanjing Museum Administration have co-organized an exhibition titled "The Gifts of the Gods: Apulia Felix Among Greeks, Indigenous and Romans". The exhibition brings together 110 sets/items of sculpture, pottery and jewelry from the collection of eight government-sponsored museums and five cultural institutions in Italy. Focusing on figures and stories from ancient Greek myths, these exquisite artifacts on display, accompanied by illustrative photos and digital installations, present the history, culture and arts that thrived for 800 years at the southernmost tip of the Apennines to the Chinese audience, conveying the Apulian pursuit of "understanding, creating and enjoying life".

致 辞

中国文物交流中心主任
谭 平

Chinese President Xi Jinping proposed the Global Civilization Initiative, emphasizing the promotion of diversity of world civilizations, the upholding of the common values shared by all humanity, and the strengthening of cultural exchanges and cooperation. This exhibition not only marks a fresh practice to enhance interchange, mutual learning and harmonious co-existence between our two civilizations, but also bears strong witness to the continuous development of China-Italy friendship through cultural exchanges. It will surely enable the audience to appreciate the unique appeal of the Greek culture and offer a gateway to perceive the human inspiration for better life.

Civilizations have become richer and more colorful with exchanges and mutual learning. Art Exhibitions China will take this exhibition as an opportunity to push the Global Civilization Initiative into practical action and work together with peers from the heritage and museum sector of the two countries to deepen exchanges and collaborations in cultural property exhibitions, promote cultural interaction and enhance people-to-people connectivity between China and Italy, and make new contributions to flourishing the garden of human civilization and building a community with a shared future for mankind.

中国和意大利是东西方文明的杰出代表。从古代丝绸之路到马可·波罗游历中国，再到传教士利玛窦翻译"四书"，两千多年的交流交往历史，使得两大文明跨越了千山万水，既彼此欣赏又相互影响。自20世纪90年代起，中国和意大利文博机构始终保持密切的展览交流。近年来，中意两国文博机构加强交往合作，中国文物交流中心持续引进意大利精品文物展到国内展出，不断丰富人民群众精神文化生活。

为了续写中意文化交流合作新篇章，中国文物交流中心与南京市博物总馆联袂引进本次展览，汇聚了八家意大利政府博物馆和五个文化机构共110余件（套）雕塑、陶器、首饰等馆藏精品，以古希腊神话人物为故事线索，结合精美图片和数码装置，将意大利亚平宁半岛南端八百年的历史、文化和艺术特色生动地呈现给观众，倾情传递普利亚人"感悟·创造·享受生活"的美好生活理念。

习近平总书记提出全球文明倡议，强调促进世界文明多样性，弘扬全人类共同价值，加强人文交流合作。此次展览不仅是两国文明交流互鉴、和合共生的生动实践，也是中意友谊在文化交流中传承发展的有力见证。

文明因交流而多彩，文明因互鉴而丰富。我们相信，通过本次展览能够让观众领略希腊文化的独特魅力和人类向往美好生活的共同愿景，促进两国民众相知相交，为世界文明多样性和不同文化交流互鉴作出新贡献！

Preface

Delegate Councilor for Culture of the Puglia Region Italy

Grazia DI BARI

The exhibition on The Gifts of the Gods - and our Puglia is full of these gifts - arises from the concept of exchange. Ancient civilizations arose and evolved from exchange. Goods, objects, artworks, values, customs, knowledge, and discoveries have been the subject of exchange. A gift is considered as such only if it is the outcome of an exchange; otherwise, it simply represents an intrinsic quality or a distinctive characteristic of a territory or a community. It doesn't become a resource. The cooperation agreement between the Puglia Region and China is founded on the ancient practice of giving and receiving, which has long characterized relations between peoples living in peace.

致　辞

意大利普利亚大区文化特派议员
格拉齐亚·迪·巴里

For the first time, universities, superintendencies, museums, and various institutions have joined forces in a virtuous and tangible collaboration, under the sponsorship of the National Museum Directorate and Archaeology, Fine Arts, and Landscape Directorate of the Italian Ministry of Culture. They have combined their expertise, qualities, and resources with a fresh and open approach to enhancing the archaeological heritage of our land, intimately and naturally linking it to the contemporary landscape of Puglia. This fruitful collaboration has given rise to the exhibition project "The Gifts of the Gods: Apulia Felix among Greeks, Indigenous people, and Romans".

The exhibition and its accompanying catalogue are not only valuable tools for study and enjoyment but also concrete proof of a shared journey between institutions for protection and research, both in Italy and China. I express my sincere gratitude to them and hope for continued participation and joint projects in the future. This is because the gifts of a land, cultural or otherwise, can truly become common goods for everyone.

"永恒的绚美——希腊时代彩陶及普利亚艺术文化特展"以及充满了众神恩赐礼物的普利亚，兴起于交流的概念。文明通过交流互鉴不断发展，无论是有形的商品、物品、艺术品，或无形的具有不同区域的风俗习惯和知识，都是交流互鉴的主体。礼物只有作为交换的结果时，才被认为是礼物。否则，它仅仅代表一片土地或一个社区的内在品质及独特特征，不会成为一种资源。普利亚大区与中国之间的合作基于给予和接受的古老习俗，这是处于和平的人们一直以来建立联系的典型方式。

在意大利国家博物馆管理局和意大利文化部考古美术及景观局的支持下，普利亚大区的大学、文化监管部门、大区各大博物馆和大区各文化机构第一次真正联合起来，进行了切实有效的合作。每个人将自己的专业知识、职业素养和资源进行整合，以新鲜、特别且开放的方法进行创意，加强了普利亚土地上的文化遗产与当代普利亚风景之间自然而亲密的联系。这次富有成果的合作最终创作出"永恒的绚美——希腊时代彩陶及普利亚艺术文化特展"。

此次展览及与展览相关画册，不仅是两国彼此学习与借鉴的宝贵工具，也是意大利和中国相关机构之间彼此分享、共同保护利用的成果展示。在此，我向双方博物馆的研究人员及工作人员表示诚挚的谢意，并希望在未来，我们能够继续合作，开展更多的项目。因为，无论是土地上、文化上还是其他方面的馈赠，都可以真正成为每个人的共同财富。

In 2018,I took Laminar of the PAULICELI family, that is the largest inheritor of Puglia to Shenzhen and made a 14-meter-high Christmas tree near "the Window of the World", the ancient carnival art is displayed in modern Shenzhen, allowing the cultural light of Puglia to shine on the land of China for the first time.In the early summer of 2019, we built 9 famous Trulli of Puglia in the central Plaza of Shenzhen Bookstore, to show Puglia's cultural and FELIX's products, also the characteristic Puglia wine PROMITIVO.

In the last six years, I have plenty times travelled and visited different cities of Puglia, As I learn more about here, I strongly want to show the value of to the land outside world.From the Italian ancient land of Puglia, to the China modern emerging city of Shenzhen, I had a profound sense of time travel, "From Antient to Futures, from the past to the future"…… how will be wonderful and exciting feeling. When I was organizing this cultural relics exhibition, I determined that we must add future parts to the ancient cultural relics exhibition. with the structure, our exhibition could be more complete. As a result, I have actually become the curator of the contemporary section of the exhibition.

Thanks to the strong support of Puglia TPP, with their assistance, I contacted with Puglia's distinctive traditional dancers and music creators who are deeply involved in ancient melodies. The Excellent photography artists and digital artists with a background in grand opera production. They gave me the materials to connect tradition and modernity, allowed my creative inspiration to become a reality.

致　辞

中国巡展总负责
洪　泉

I would like to express my special thanks to Mrs. Di Bari, the cultural representative of the Puglia region. Thank you for coming to Nanjing and providing strong support in our difficult time. I would give big thanks to Mr. Aldo PATRUNO, Director of the Ministry of Tourism, Culture, Economy and Territorial Development. Thanks for your understanding and support especially during the epidemic when our projects could not be carried out on time.I would also like to express my thanks to the Science Committee team. Over the past three years, as a professional and serious team, thank for professional and strong support.

Thanks to the Art Exhbitions China, with your powerful support and effective control can the exhibition be successfully held in China.Finally, thank you to Nanjing Museum Administration and the Oriental Metropolitan Museum(the 3rd-6th century), professional planning, beautiful design, wonderful media promotion, made our exhibition attractive and full of the education knowledge.

There is a long way to go, let us Taking the exhibition as a new beginning, continue to explore the culture road of Italy and China.

2018 年，我带着普利亚光雕的最大传承人保利切利家族制作的光雕，在深圳世界之窗附近打造了高 14 米的圣诞树，古老的嘉年华艺术，在现代化的深圳得以展现，让普利亚的文化之光，第一次闪现在中国的土地上。同年初夏，我们在中国最大的书城深圳书城的中心大堂建立了 9 座普利亚最著名的特鲁利建筑，展示普利亚的文化风情、丰饶的物产及特色的普利亚普里米蒂沃美酒。

六年里，近百次穿行于普利亚不同的古城中，当我更多地了解这里，我更加想把这里的价值展现给外面的世界。从古老的意大利普利亚大地，到中国代表未来的现代新兴城市深圳，让我有时光穿梭的感觉，也让我意识到了"从古代到未来，从过去到未来"，是一个多么美妙而不可思议的过程。伴随着这样的体会，我在组织此次文物展览的时候，确信必须在古老的文物展览中加入未来的部分，只有这样的架构，才能让我们的展览更加完整。由此，我也真正成了此次展览当代部分的策展人。

感谢普利亚博物馆联盟的大力支持，在他们的协助下，我有幸接触到充满普利亚特色的传统舞蹈家、深耕古旋律的音乐创作家、足迹走遍世界的优秀摄影艺术家、拥有大歌剧制作背景的艺术家，是他们给了我将传统与现代结合到一起的素材，也让我的创意灵感变成了现实。

我要特别感谢普利亚大区文化代表议员迪·巴里女士，感谢你亲临南京，在我们困难的时刻，提供强有力的支持。我也要特别感谢普利亚大区文化旅游与领土部部长阿尔多·帕特鲁诺先生，自 2018 年至今，感谢你一路的理解与支持，特别是在疫情期间，我们的项目不能按时进行。我也要特别感谢此次展览的意大利学术委员会团队，三年来，作为专业的团队，感谢你们在幕后默默而强大地支持着展览。

感谢中国文物交流中心，你们的大力支持与有效把控，让展览得以在中国完美举办。最后感谢南京市博物总馆、六朝博物馆，你们专业的策划、唯美的展陈设计、深化的推广，让展览被观众喜爱，成为一个非常有教育意义的展览。

我们还有很长的路要走，让我们以此次展览为新起点，继续探索意大利与中国之间的文化交流之路。

Preface

The Oriental Metropolitan Museum (The 3rd-6th century) Director of General Business Department
Zhang Lei

The exhibition perfectly interprets the past and future of Puglia. In addition to the display of exquisite colored pottery, sculptures, coins and other cultural relics, it also shows digital artworks created by Italian artists, pictures of Puglia's natural scenery, cultural heritage and Carnival landscape. During the exhibition period in Nanjing, the exhibition attracted 350,000 visitors, with a total of 85 articles published in the media and the museum's WeChat, and more than 56 million readers of online information.

Since September 2022, we have approached the Art Exhbitions China with the intention of the exhibition, and after the exhibition was approved for the project, we communicated with the Italian side of the museum staff and archaeologists online. We communicated with domestic scholars and translators to refine words in the text of the exhibition. After determining the logic between the levels of the exhibition, we completed the finalization of the text of the exhibition content. We confirmed the exhibition of cultural relics repeatedly. Six months before the exhibition, we communicated with the teams from all sides almost every day. We've discussed and communicated it over and over again,communication is a necessary way to work innovation and realize mutual recognition.

After an in-depth analysis of the content, we started to discuss with the exhibition design team uninterruptedly, to conceptualize how to connect the theme space with a storyline, and to determine the visiting line, spatial scenario, color tone of the exhibition hall and highlight areas. After the desgn program is finalized, we need to keep track of the project's progress and construction quality during the exhibition production stage. After that, we need to plan and prepare for the poster exhibition, AR online exhibition, receive media interviews, conceive, write and proofread publicity texts, organize and carry out interpretation services and social education activities, all of which need to be detailed and implemented.

After the completion of the exhibition design and production, some highlight elements in the exhibition hall have become the card points for the audience to take photos, such as the

致 辞

六朝博物馆综合业务部主任
张 蕾

columns at the entrance, the round arch in the sculpture area, the banquet and music and dance scenes, the experience space of the mirror house, an the photo art display device, and so on. We ensure the safety of the cultural relics at the site of point handover, coordination of filming and recording and other related work in the cultural relics point handover and exhibition link, so that the cultural relics can be presented in the most beautiful posture through the sense of rhythm and rhythmic beauty of the display. We need to repeatedly adjust the angle and position of the exhibits and control the details. In one corner of the exhibition hall, we have also designed an exhibit touch zone for the visually impaired. There is no ultimate perfection in the exhibition, only the persistence of details.

From the planning and the opening to the withdrawal of the exhibition, the members of the curatorial teams of China and Italy who participated in the work of the exhibition were all concerned with the exhibition and devoted themselves to it. Visitors to the Oriental Metropolitan Museum (the 3rd-6th Century) can feel the diversified interaction and exchange and development of world cultures through the exhibition, thus deepening cultural identity, ethnic identity and national identity. We believe that this exhibition held in Nanjing in the summer of 2023, which brought us cultural longing and aesthetic touch, will be long remembered in the hearts of the audience and participants.

展览完美诠释了普利亚的过去与未来，除展示精美彩陶、雕塑、钱币等文物外，同时展示了意大利艺术家们创作的数码艺术作品，普利亚自然风光、文化遗产和嘉年华景观图片。在南京展出期间，吸引到35万观众前来参观，媒体报道及馆方微信发布文章累计85篇，网络信息阅读量逾5600万人次。

2022年9月，我们与中国文物交流中心意向接洽。展览获批立项后，又与意大利方博物馆工作人员和考古学家线上沟通，与国内学者及翻译人员就展览文字反复磨合。在确定展览逻辑线后，我们完成了展览文字定稿，并对展出文物反复确认。展览开展前半年，几乎每天都在与各方团队沟通、碰撞、再沟通。沟通，成为展览创新和实现相互认同的必要途径。

在对内容深入解析后，我们开始与展陈设计团队探讨和构思如何以故事线串联主题空间、确定参观动线、空间场景、展厅色调及亮点区域等。设计方案确定后，展陈制作阶段持续跟进工程进度与施工质量。包括策划筹备海报展、AR线上展览，接待媒体采访，酝酿宣传文字、审校，组织开展讲解服务和社教活动等，每项工作都需要细化、落实。

展陈制作完成后，展厅内一些亮点元素成为观众留影的打卡点，例如入口处的立柱、雕塑区的圆形拱门、宴饮及乐舞场景、镜屋体验空间以及艺术图片展示装置等。在点交和布展环节，我们通过有节奏感和韵律美的布陈让文物能够以最美姿态呈现，并保障现场文物安全、协调文物拍摄工作等。展品布陈时的角度和位置调整、细节把控、重复再重复。在展厅一角，我们为视障人士设计了展品触摸区。展览没有极致的完美，只有对细节的执着。

从策划、开幕到撤展，参与展览工作的中意两国策展团队工作人员均心系展览，倾力付出。来六朝博物馆参观的观众，通过此次观展体验，感受到世界文化的多元互动和交流发展，从而加深文化认同、民族认同和国家认同。相信这场2023年夏天在南京举办、带给我们文化憧憬和审美触动的展览，会在观众和工作人员心中长久铭记。

希腊时代彩陶及
普利亚艺术文化特展

永恒的绚美

THE GIFTS
OF
THE GODS

APULIA FELIX AMONG GREEKS

INDIGENOUS AND ROMANS

Hosts	主　办
Nanjing Museum Administration	南京市博物总馆
Art Exhibitions China	中国文物交流中心
Poli Biblio-Museali della Regione Puglia Italia	意大利普利亚博物馆联盟

Organizers	承　办
The Oriental Metropolitan Museum（The 3rd-6th century）	六朝博物馆
Shenzhen PLD Marketing Planning Co., Ltd.	深圳市普兰迪营销策划有限公司

Support	支持单位
Italian Ministry of Culture	意大利文化部

目 录
Contents

Museums are important sanctuaries to safeguard and transmit human civilization and bridges to connect the past, the present, and the future, playing a special role in promoting exchanges and mutual learning among civilizations. Nanjing is a historical and cultural city and a city of museums. Since its establishment, Nanjing Museum Administration has adopted the "bring in and go global" strategy and kept exploring new ground to provide a platform for exchanges among different cultures and clashes among different viewpoints. We will display "The Gifts of the Gods: Apulia Felix Among Greeks, Indigenous and Romans", an exhibition introduced in collaboration with Art Exhibitions China, with loans provided by eight museums from Italy.

Since the ancient Greek times, the sea has long been the foundation for the economic and cultural development of the Mediterranean. The sea has brought not only abundant marine resources but also prosperous marine trade for Puglia in the south of Italy, a core area in the Mediterranean. While people lived and worked in peace and comfort, they spread myths and legends of the Greek gods far and wide in this land which became part of their daily lives. Today, Puglia is still a must-to-go place for young Westerners to understand ancient Greece and experience beautiful lives.

The exhibition is curated on the basis of six gods in ancient Greek myths and intended to present scenarios of art, culture, commerce and agriculture in Puglia through the display of exquisite potteries, sculptures and coins. Among the brilliant cultural legacies from ancient Greece, colored pottery is the most capturing, whose designs of human figures and their surroundings are closely associated with society and life of ancient Greece.

前　言
Foreword

While Chinese civilization enjoys a time-honored history, ancient Greek civilization has a far-reaching impact.

We hope that the first leg of the travelling exhibition in Nanjing, for the purpose of promoting interchange between East and West civilizations, would contribute to our vision to build Nanjing Museum Administration and the Oriental Metropolitan Museum（the 3rd-6th century） into a major platform for exchanges and mutual learning among civilizations.

We hope that the exhibition, showcasing the essence of ancient Greek civilization and presenting national memory and vitality with the display of fantastic collections and photos, would help enlighten our mind and broaden our vision.

We also hope that the exhibition, expressing curatorial ideas of Chinese and Italian parties, would offer positive guidance on modern aesthetics and cultural understanding and serve as a bridge to facilitate exchanges and dialogue between Chinese and Western civilizations.

博物馆作为保护和传承人类文明的重要殿堂，是连接过去、现在、未来的桥梁，在促进世界文明交流互鉴方面具有特殊作用。南京是历史文化名城，也是博物馆之城。南京市博物总馆自成立以来，"走出去，引进来"，开拓创新，为不同文化的交流、不同观点的碰撞提供平台。此次，中国文物交流中心引进"永恒的绚美——希腊时代彩陶及普利亚艺术文化特展"，由意大利八家博物馆提供藏品支持。

自古希腊时代起，海洋就是地中海区域经济文化发展的基础。意大利南部的普利亚是地中海的核心区域，海洋为其带来丰富的海产，让这里的海洋贸易蓬勃发展。在人们安居乐业的同时，希腊众神的故事在这片土地上不断传颂，与人们的生活紧密联系。直至今日，普利亚依然是西方年轻人"感悟古希腊，感受绚美生活"的必去之处。

展览以古希腊神话中的六位神祇作为组织展品的故事线索，通过陶器、雕塑、钱币等精美文物，呈现普利亚地区的艺术、文化、商业、农业等风貌。在璀璨的古希腊文化遗产中，彩陶最为引人注目，彩陶上所描绘的人物形象及周围环境均与古希腊社会生活息息相关。

中华文明源远流长，古希腊文明影响深远。

希望以促进东西方文明融合为宗旨的此次巡展，在南京的首站首秀，能够助力南京市博物总馆、六朝博物馆成为中外文化交流互鉴的媒介。

希望代表古希腊文明精髓及以藏品和图片共同呈现民族记忆和活力的本次展览，能够启迪心灵，开阔视野。

希望本次展览能充分表达中意团队策展理念，对现代艺术审美、文化感知起到正向引导作用，成为东西文明碰撞与交流的桥梁。

普利亚
Introduction of Apulia

Apulia is the Italian extreme offshoot of a long peninsula towards the East , in the heart of the Mediterranean. The Italian territory is like a female high heeled boot, it is the heel of the "boot".Thanks to its position, it has received continuous contributions from many different civilizations over the millennia, representing a complex and original mix of cultures and civilizations.

In the first millennium BEC, it was divided into three parts: Daunia in the north, Peucezia in the centre, and Messapia in the south.The three parts were warlike societies, highly evolved articulated, endowed with a rich agrarian economy, in a relationship of conflict but also of exchange and integration with the Greek world,in particular with the only Greek colony, founded at the end of the 8th century BC by colonists from Sparta, Taras (today Taranto).

Between the end of the 4th century BEC and the lst century BEC, Apulia was conquered by Rome and became part of the Roman Empire. The monuments,objects and traces of these ancient civilizations are today part of the culture, cities and landscapes of contemporary Apulia.

普利亚是意大利向东方延伸的最远分支，位于地中海中心。意大利版图如同一只女性高跟靴，普利亚就是"靴子"的后跟。得益于其地理位置，数千年来，它不断接受来自不同文明的贡献，代表着复杂而原始的文化和文明的融合。

公元前 1000 年，它被分为三个部分：北部的道尼亚（Daunia）、中部的普乌西蒂亚（Peucezia）和南部的梅萨皮亚（Messapia）。这三部分，高度发展且相互衔接，拥有丰富的农业经济，与希腊世界，特别是与公元前 8 世纪末由斯巴达殖民者建立的唯一希腊殖民地塔拉斯（今塔兰托）之间交流和融合。

公元前 4 世纪末至公元前 1 世纪，普利亚被罗马征服，成为罗马帝国的一部分。这些古代文明的遗迹、物品和痕迹如今已成为当代普利亚文化、城市和景观的一部分。

本章以六位古希腊神祇为线索，

通过陶器、雕塑、钱币等精美文物，

展示普利亚于公元前 6 世纪

至公元 2 世纪，

800 年间精湛的工艺技术

与人们丰富的心灵生活。

In this unit, six ancient Greek deities serve as guiding concepts that bind together a range of exquisitely crafted objects demonstrating the rich spiritual life of Apulia during the 800-year period (6th century BEC to the 2nd century CE), including terracotta vessels and objects, sculpture, and coins.

希腊神话与文物

Greek Myths and Artifacts

1

Section 1-1

波塞冬

海洋与资源

Poseidon

GOD OF THE SEA
AND
RESOURCES

波塞冬是古希腊神话中的海洋之神，是与海洋相关一切职业的主宰神。对于意大利南部居民而言，海洋既神秘又富饶。这里展示的彩陶、雕塑等珍贵的文物将神话与现实相结合，展现出独特的海洋印象。

Poseidon is the god of the sea in ancient Greek mythology and the ruler of all professions related to the ocean. For the inhabitants of southern Italy, the sea is both mysterious and abundant. The precious artifacts showcased here, such as vase paintings and sculptures, blend mythology with reality, presenting a unique impression of the ocean.

普利亚式红绘双耳酒瓶

公元前 360 – 前 340 年

塔兰托国家考古博物馆藏

Apulian red-Figure pelike

360 BCE - 340 BCE

National Archaeological Museum of Taranto (MArTA)

海豚骑手塔拉斯陶俑

公元前 4 世纪

塔兰托国家考古博物馆藏

Terracotta figurine depicting Taras riding a dolphin

4th century BCE

National Archaeological Museum of Taranto (MArTA)

陶质祭坛

公元前 4 世纪下半叶

塔兰托国家考古博物馆藏

Terracotta arula (Portable altar)

Second half of the 4th century BCE

National Archaeological Museum of Taranto (MArTA)

海豚形象大理石雕残件

公元前 1 世纪 – 1 世纪

塔兰托国家考古博物馆藏

Marble furniture fragment depicting a dolphin

1st century BCE - 1st century CE

National Archaeological Museum of Taranto (MArTA)

塞壬形象陶质香精瓶

公元前 6 世纪中期
塔兰托国家考古博物馆藏

Terracott balsamarium configured as a Siren

Mid-6th century BCE
National Archaeological Museum of Taranto (MArTA)

海仙女乘坐"鱼尾马人"陶塑群像

公元前 2 世纪下半叶
塔兰托国家考古博物馆藏

Polychrome terracotta group depicting a Nereid on an ichthyo centaur

Second half of the 2nd century BCE

National Archaeological Museum of Taranto (MArTA)

普利亚红绘女妖斯库拉角杯

公元前 350 – 前 340 年

雅达博物馆藏

Apulian red-figure rhyton shaped as Scylla

350 BCE - 340 BCE

Jatta National Archaeological Museum, Ruvo di Puglia

小神庙式墓葬石质浮雕残块

公元前 3 世纪

塔兰托国家考古博物馆藏

Fragment of a relief in soft stone belonging to a small temple-shaped funerary monument (Naiskos)

3rd century BCE

National Archaeological Museum of Taranto (MArTA)

双口白陶瓶

公元前 3 世纪

西吉斯蒙多 - 卡斯特罗梅迪亚诺博物馆藏

Askos listato

3rd century BCE

Sigismondo Castromediano Museum, Lecce

坎帕尼亚红绘鱼盘

公元前 4 世纪
塔兰托国家考古博物馆藏

Campanian red-figure fish plate

4th century BCE
National Archaeological Museum of Taranto (MArTA)

普利亚红绘鱼盘

公元前 350 - 前 340 年

塔兰托国家考古博物馆藏

Apulian red figure fish plate

350 BCE - 340 BCE

National Archaeological Museum of Taranto (MArTA)

普利亚红绘斟酒壶

公元前 4 世纪中期
塔兰托国家考古博物馆藏

Apulian red-figure oinochoe

Mid-4th century BCE
National Archaeological Museum of Taranto (MArTA)

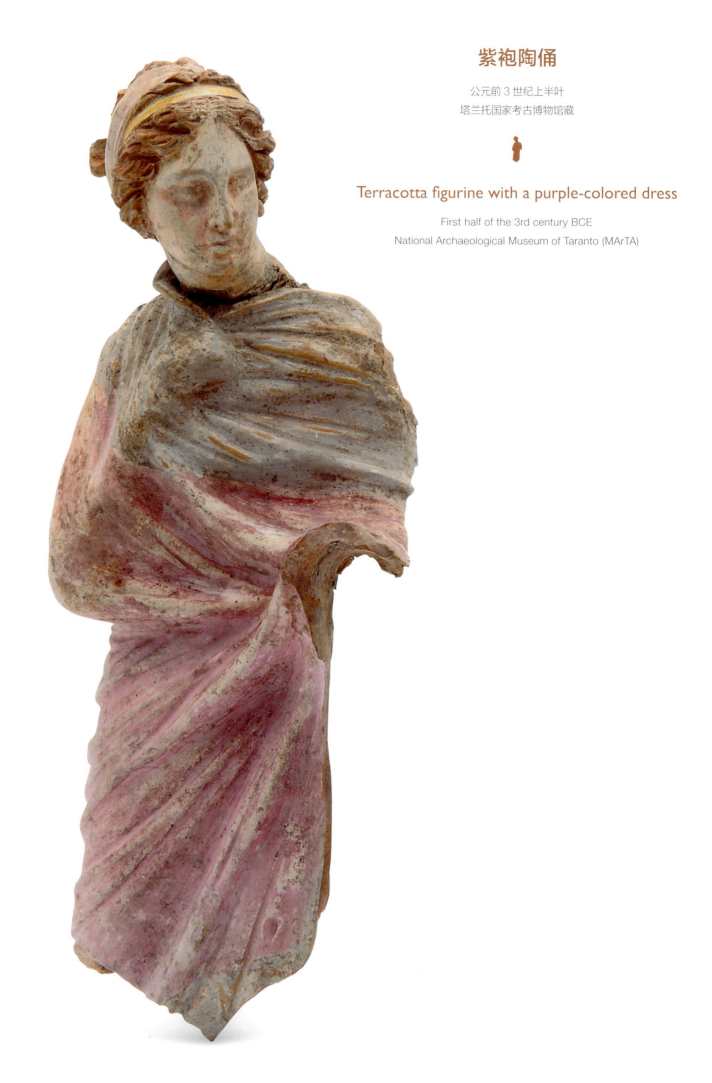

紫袍陶俑

公元前 3 世纪上半叶
塔兰托国家考古博物馆藏

Terracotta figurine with a purple-colored dress

First half of the 3rd century BCE
National Archaeological Museum of Taranto (MArTA)

拉孔尼亚浅口杯

公元前 580 – 前 570 年
塔兰托国家考古博物馆藏

Laconian kylix

580 BCE - 570 BCE
National Archaeological Museum of Taranto (MArTA)

银币

公元前 4 世纪 - 前 3 世纪晚期
塔兰托国家考古博物馆藏

Silver coin

4th century BCE - late 3rd century BCE
National Archaeological Museum of Taranto (MArTA)

德墨忒耳

粮食与丰饶

Demeter

GRAIN
AND ABUNDANCE

德墨忒耳是古希腊神话中的农业与生育女神。希腊人将农作物的繁荣与收获归功于她。古希腊瓶画中常见德墨忒耳派特里普托勒摩斯为世界引介谷物的故事。普利亚地区从新石器时代起就是重要的农业产区，德墨忒耳相关的崇拜仪式至今在当地的习俗中仍然可见。

Demeter is the goddess of agriculture and fertility in ancient Greek mythology. The Greeks attributed the prosperity and harvest of crops to Demeter. In ancient Greek vase paintings, it is common to see depictions of Demeter introducing grains to the world, often accompanied by Triptolemos. The region of Apulia has been an important agricultural area since the Neolithic period, and the worship of Demeter and related rituals can still be seen in local customs and cuisine to this day.

德墨忒耳半身像

公元前 5 世纪

西吉斯蒙多 - 卡斯特罗梅迪亚诺博物馆藏

Half-length statue relief of Demeter

5th century BCE

Sigismondo Castromediano Museum, Lecce

陶质女性半身像

公元前 4 世纪末 – 前 3 世纪初
塔兰托国家考古博物馆藏

Terracotta female protome-bust

Late 4th century BCE - early 3rd century BCE
National Archaeological Museum of Taranto (MArTA)

持四角火炬女性像陶模

公元前 4 世纪下半叶
塔兰托国家考古博物馆藏

Terracotta mold of a female figurine with a four-armed torch

Second half of the 4th century BCE

National Archaeological Museum of Taranto (MArTA)

普利亚红绘盘

公元前 365 - 前 350 年

雅达博物馆藏

Apulian red-figure plate

365 BCE - 350 BCE

Jatta National Archaeological Museum, Ruvo di Puglia

小神庙式墓葬建筑雕像部件

公元前 3 世纪
塔兰托国家考古博物馆藏

Sculpture of a funerary monument (Naiskos)

3rd century BCE
National Archaeological Museum of Taranto (MArTA)

阿提卡红绘柱耳调酒缸

公元前 440 - 前 430 年
里贝佐布林迪西博物馆藏

Attic red-figure column krater

440 BCE - 430 BCE
Ribezzo Archaeological Museum, Brindisi

银币

公元前 400 – 前 340 年

塔兰托国家考古博物馆藏

Silver coin

400 BCE - 340 BCE

National Archaeological Museum of Taranto (MArTA)

陶质献礼盘印模

公元前 4 世纪
塔兰托国家考古博物馆藏

Mold of a terracotta votive disc

4th century BCE
National Archaeological Museum of Taranto (MArTA)

陶质石榴

公元前 6 世纪
塔兰托国家考古博物馆藏

Terracotta pomegranate

6th century BCE
National Archaeological Museum of Taranto (MArTA)

陶质小乳猪沙铃

公元前 4 世纪
塔兰托国家考古博物馆藏

Terracotta piglet rattle

4th century BCE
National Archaeological Museum of Taranto (MArTA)

小乳猪形陶质沙铃

公元前 4 世纪 – 前 3 世纪

西吉斯蒙多 – 卡斯特罗梅迪亚诺博物馆藏

Small pig-shaped terracotta rattle (Tintinnabula)

4th century BCE - 3rd century BCE

Sigismondo Castromediano Museum, Lecce

陶质罂粟壳

公元前 4 世纪 – 前 3 世纪
塔兰托国家考古博物馆藏

Terracotta poppy seed pod

4th century BCE - 3rd century BCE
National Archaeological Museum of Taranto (MArTA)

雅典娜

橄榄树、橄榄油、手工艺

Athena

OLIVE TREE, OLIVE OIL, AND CRAFTS

雅典娜是古希腊神话中的战争女神、智慧女神。她脱胎自神王宙斯的头颅，在打败海神波塞冬后成为雅典城邦的主神。雅典娜变出橄榄树，给人们带来希望与和平，橄榄树的果实和橄榄油可用于点灯、疗伤、保持健康。

Athena is the goddess of war and wisdom in ancient Greek mythology. She was born fully grown from the head of Zeus and became the patron goddess of the city-state of Athens after defeating the sea god Poseidon. Athena is associated with the olive tree, which she created, symbolizing hope and peace. The fruit of the olive tree and its oil have various uses, such as lighting lamps, healing wounds, and maintaining good health. Additionally, Athena is also associated with craftsmanship and is revered as a protector and inspiration for artisans and craftsmen.

雅典娜大理石雕像（复制品）

西吉斯蒙多－卡斯特罗梅迪亚诺博物馆藏

Replica of the marble statue of Athena

Sigismondo Castromediano Museum, Lecce

阿提卡白底式油瓶

公元前 500 – 前 475 年
塔兰托国家考古博物馆藏

Attic White-ground Lekythos

500 BCE - 475 BCE

National Archaeological Museum of Taranto (MArTA)

陶质圆形置物盒

公元前 4 世纪 – 前 3 世纪

西吉斯蒙多 – 卡斯特罗梅迪亚诺博物馆藏

Circular terracotta container (Pyxis)

4th century BCE -3rd century BCE

Sigismondo Castromediano Museum, Lecce

铜质油灯

公元 2 世纪 – 3 世纪

西吉斯蒙多 – 卡斯特罗梅迪亚诺博物馆

Bronze oil lamp

2nd century CE - 3rd century CE

Sigismondo Castromediano Museum, Lecce

陶质油灯

公元前 1 世纪 – 1 世纪
西吉斯蒙多 – 卡斯特罗梅迪亚诺博物馆藏

Terracotta oil lamp

1st century BCE - 1st century CE
Sigismondo Castromediano Museum, Lecce

亚红绘萼形调酒缸

公元前 430 – 前 400 年

西吉斯蒙多 – 卡斯特罗梅迪亚诺博物馆藏

Apulian red-figure calyx krater

430 BCE - 400 BCE

Sigismondo Castromediano Museum, Lecce

卢坎尼亚红绘调酒缸

公元前 380 – 前 360 年
西吉斯蒙多 – 卡斯特罗梅迪亚诺博物馆藏

Lucanian red-figure calyx krater

380 BCE - 360 BCE
Sigismondo Castromediano Museum, Lecce

陶质纺锤

公元前 4 世纪
雅达博物馆藏

Terracotta spindle

4th century BCE
Jatta National Archaeological Museum, Ruvo di Puglia

普利亚红绘钟形调酒缸

公元前 425 - 前 400 年
雅达博物馆藏

Apulian red-figure bell krater

425 BCE - 400 BCE

Jatta National Archaeological Museum, Ruvo di Puglia

普利亚红绘圆盘

公元前 4 世纪中期

雅达博物馆藏

Apulian red-figure kylix

Mid-4th century BCE

Jatta National Archaeological Museum, Ruvo di Puglia

猫头鹰图像双耳杯

公元前 5 世纪末 – 前 4 世纪初

塔兰托国家考古博物馆藏

Owl image skyphos

Late 5th century BCE - early 4th century BCE

National Archaeological Museum of Taranto (MArTA)

雅典娜雕塑

塔兰托国家考古博物馆藏

Athena sculpture

National Archaeological Museum of Taranto (MArTA)

狄俄尼索斯

美酒与宴饮

Dionysus

GOD OF WINE AND FESTIVITY

狄俄尼索斯是古希腊神话中的酒神和狂欢之神。他是唯一一位人神结合所生，却位列奥林波斯十二主神的神祇。他是"最甜蜜"，也"最令凡人畏怖的神灵" ——美酒予人欢乐，同时降下毁灭的暴力。

Dionysus is the god of wine and revelry in Greek mythology. He is the only god born from the union of a mortal and a god, yet he is counted among the twelve Olympian gods. He is both the "most delightful" and the "most terrifying of the gods": wine brings joy to people, but it can also unleash destructive violence.

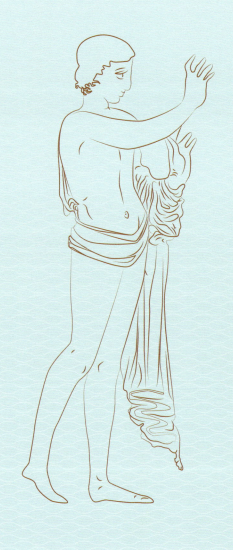

普利亚钟形调酒缸

公元前 3 世纪

西吉斯蒙多－卡斯特罗梅迪亚诺博物馆藏

Apulian Polychrome bell krater

3rd century BCE

Sigismondo Castromediano Museum, Lecce

普利亚红绘调酒缸

公元前 400 – 前 375 年

西吉斯蒙多 – 卡斯特罗梅迪亚诺博物馆藏

Apulian red-figure krater

400BCE - 375 BCE

Sigismondo Castromediano Museum, Lecce

覆彩式彩釉陶盆

公元前 330 – 前 320 年
里贝佐布林迪西博物馆藏

Overpainted polychrome basin

330 BCE - 320 BCE
Ribezzo Archaeological Museum, Brindisi

普利亚红绘调酒缸

公元前 400 - 前 375 年

西吉斯蒙多 - 卡斯特罗梅迪亚诺博物馆藏

Apulian red-figure krater

400 BCE - 375 BCE

Sigismondo Castromediano Museum, Lecce

普利亚红绘双耳瓶

公元前 370 – 前 340 年
圣塞巴斯提安诺考古文物储藏中心藏

Apulian red-figure polychrome hydria

370 BCE - 340 BCE
Archaeological Heritage Storage Center of San Severo, Gravina in Puglia

普利亚红绘钟形调酒缸

公元前 3 世纪
圣塞巴斯提安诺考古文物储藏中心藏

Apulian red-figure bell-krater

3rd century BCE
Archaeological Heritage Storage Center of San Severo, Gravina in Puglia

阿提卡黑绘斟酒壶

公元前 6 世纪末
巴里市考古、美术和景观监管局藏

Attic black-figure oinochoe (Wine jug)

Late 6th century BCE
Archaeological Site and Landscape Supervision Office, Bari (SABAP)

黑绘柱耳调酒缸

公元前 6 世纪
巴里市考古、美术和景观监管局藏

Attic black-figure column krater

6th century BCE
Archaeological Site and Landscape Supervision Office, Bari (SABAP)

大眼浅口高足杯

公元前 510 – 前 470 年
巴里市考古、美术和景观监管局藏

Eye-cup (Kylix)

510 BCE - 470 BCE

Archaeological Site and Landscape Supervision Office, Bari (SABAP)

阿提卡黑绘深口翘耳杯

公元前 5 世纪 – 前 4 世纪
巴里市考古、美术和景观监管局藏

Attic black-figure deep bowl with upturned handles (Skyphos)

5th century BCE - 4th century BCE

Archaeological Site and Landscape Supervision Office, Bari (SABAP)

普利亚红绘钟形调酒缸

公元前 360 – 前 340 年

西吉斯蒙多－卡斯特罗梅迪亚诺博物馆藏

Apulian red-figure bell krater

360 BCE - 340 BCE

Sigismondo Castromediano Museum, Lecce

普利亚红绘钟形调酒缸

公元前 375 – 前 325 年

圣塞巴斯提安诺考古文物储藏中心藏

Apulian red-figure bell krater

375 BCE - 325 BCE

San Sebastiano Archaeological Operations Center Storage, Gravina in Puglia

阿提卡红绘柱耳调酒缸

公元前 480 – 前 450 年

巴里市考古、美术和景观监管局藏

Attic red-figure column krater

480 BCE - 450 BCE

Archaeological Site and Landscape Supervision Office, Bari (SABAP)

红绘浅口杯

公元前 5 世纪下半叶
圣塞巴斯提安诺考古文物储藏中心藏

Red-figure kylix

Second half of the 5th century BCE
San Sebastiano Archaeological Operations Center Storage, Gravina in Puglia

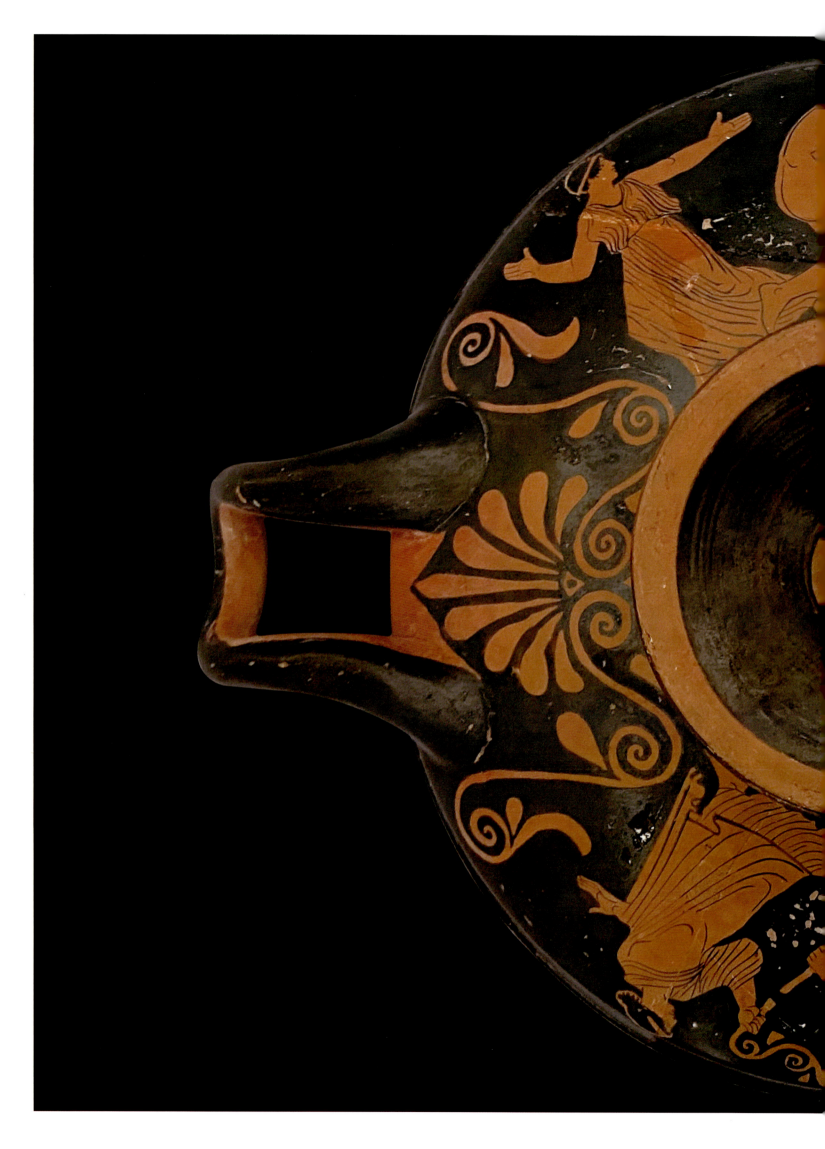

红绘萼形调酒缸

公元前 4 世纪初

阿尔塔穆拉国家考古博物馆藏

Red-figure calyx krater

Early 4th century BCE

National Archaeological Museum of Altamura

肉类烹煮金属锅具

公元前 5 世纪下半叶
巴里市考古、美术和景观监管局藏

Metal cookware for meat preparation

Second half of the 5th century BCE
Archaeological Site and Landscape Supervision Office, Bari (SABAP)

调酒缸

公元前 5 世纪末 – 前 4 世纪初

圣塞巴斯提安诺考古文物储藏中心藏

Krater

End of the 5th century BCE - beginning of the 4th century BCE

San Sebastiano Archaeological Operations Center Storage, Gravina in Puglia

酒壶

公元前 4 世纪上半叶
圣塞巴斯提安诺考古文物储藏中心藏

Wine jug (Oinochoe)

First half of the 4th BCE
San Sebastiano Archaeological Operations Center Storage, Gravina in Puglia

饮酒杯

公元前 4 世纪
圣塞巴斯提安诺考古文物储藏中心藏

Drinking cup (Skyphos)

4th century BCE
San Sebastiano Archaeological Operations Center
Storage, Gravina in Puglia

饮酒杯

公元前 4 世纪上半叶
圣塞巴斯提安诺考古文物储藏中心藏

Drinking cup (Skyphos)

First half of the 4th century BCE
San Sebastiano Archaeological Operations Center
Storage, Gravina in Puglia

宴饮盘

公元前 4 世纪
圣塞巴斯提安诺考古文物储藏中心藏

Banquet plate (Patera)

4th century BCE
San Sebastiano Archaeological Operations Center Storage, Gravina in Puglia

单耳杯

公元前 4 世纪

圣塞巴斯提安诺考古文物储藏中心藏

Single-handled cup

4th century BCE

San Sebastiano Archaeological Operations Center Storage, Gravina in Puglia

宴饮壶

公元前 5 世纪末 - 前 4 世纪初
圣塞巴斯提安诺考古文物储藏中心藏

Wine jug (Olpe)

End of the 5th century BCE - beginning of the 4th BCE
San Sebastiano Archaeological Operations Center Storage, Gravina in Puglia

道尼亚式环耳杯

公元前 4 世纪上半叶
圣塞巴斯提安诺考古文物储藏中心藏

Daunian style kanatharos

First half of the 4th century BCE
San Sebastiano Archaeological Operations Center Storage, Gravina in Puglia

单耳杯

公元前 4 世纪上半叶
圣塞巴斯提安诺考古文物储藏中心藏

Single-handled cup (Coppa)

First half of the 4th century BCE
San Sebastiano Archaeological Operations Center Storage, Gravina in Puglia

宴饮碗

公元前 4 世纪上半叶
圣塞巴斯提安诺考古文物储藏中心藏

Cup (Coppa)

First half of the 4th century BCE
San Sebastiano Archaeological Operations Center Storage, Gravina in Puglia

压印浅杯

公元前 4 世纪上半叶

圣塞巴斯提安诺考古文物储藏中心藏

Stamped shallow cup (Kylix)

First half of the 4th century BCE

San Sebastiano Archaeological Operations Center Storage, Gravina in Puglia

矮人负鹤红绘角杯

公元前 460 – 前 450 年
巴里市考古、美术和景观监管局藏

Red-figure rhyton depicting a pygmy dragging a crane by the neck

460 BCE - 450 BCE
Archaeological Site and Landscape Supervision Office, Bari (SABAP)

双耳深口环耳杯

公元前 5 世纪中叶

巴里市考古、美术和景观监管局藏

Kantharos of Saint Valentin type

Mid-5th century BCE

Archaeological Site and Landscape Supervision Office, Bari (SABAP)

女性头像酒壶

公元前 5 世纪

巴里市考古、美术和景观监管局藏

Oinochoe shaped as a female head

5th century BCE

Archaeological Site and Landscape Supervision Office, Bari (SABAP)

大型贸易双耳瓶

公元前 1 世纪
里贝佐布林迪西博物馆藏

Large trade amphora

1st century BCE

Ribezzo Archaeological Museum, Brindisi

普利亚红绘篮形调酒缸

公元前 370 - 前 350 年

西吉斯蒙多 - 卡斯特罗梅迪亚诺博物馆藏

Apulian red-figure calyx krater

370 BCE - 350 BCE

Sigismondo Castromediano Museum, Lecce

红绘杯形调酒缸

公元前 4 世纪

西吉斯蒙多 – 卡斯特罗梅迪亚诺博物馆藏

Red-figure polychrome chalice krater

4th century BCE

Sigismondo Castromediano Museum, Lecce

阿波罗是古希腊神话中的光明之神、音乐之神、预言之神和医疗之神。其标志性乐器是竖琴，被视作代表理性的乐器。他是人类诗歌音乐的灵感来源，为人类带来多种多样的幸福感。

阿波罗

音乐与艺术

Apollo

GOD OF MUSIC AND ART

Apollo is the god of light, music, prophecy, and healing in ancient Greek mythology. His iconic instrument is the lyre, which is considered a symbol of rationality. He is the source of inspiration for human poetry and music, bringing various forms of happiness to humanity.

阿提卡黑绘油瓶

公元前 500 – 前 475 年
西吉斯蒙多 – 卡斯特罗梅迪亚诺博物馆藏

Attic black-figure oil flask (Lekythos)

500 BCE - 475 BCE
Sigismondo Castromediano Museum, Lecce

阿提卡红绘浅口杯

公元前 5 世纪
巴里市考古、美术和景观监管局藏

Attic red-figure shallow cup (Kylix)

5th century BCE
Archaeological Site and Landscape Supervision Office, Bari (SABAP)

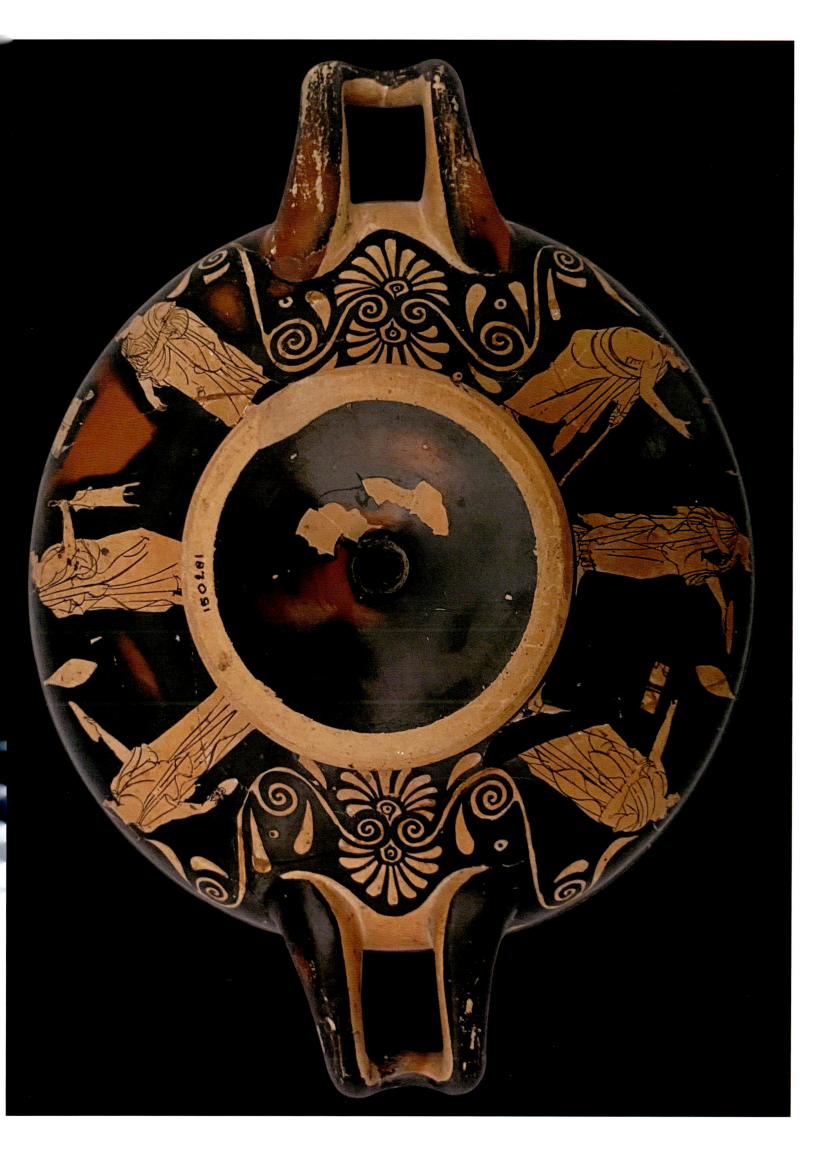

红绘蜷耳调酒缸

公元前 5 世纪
巴里市考古、美术和景观监管局藏

Red-figure volute krater

5th century BCE
Archaeological Site and Landscape Supervision Office, Bari (SABAP)

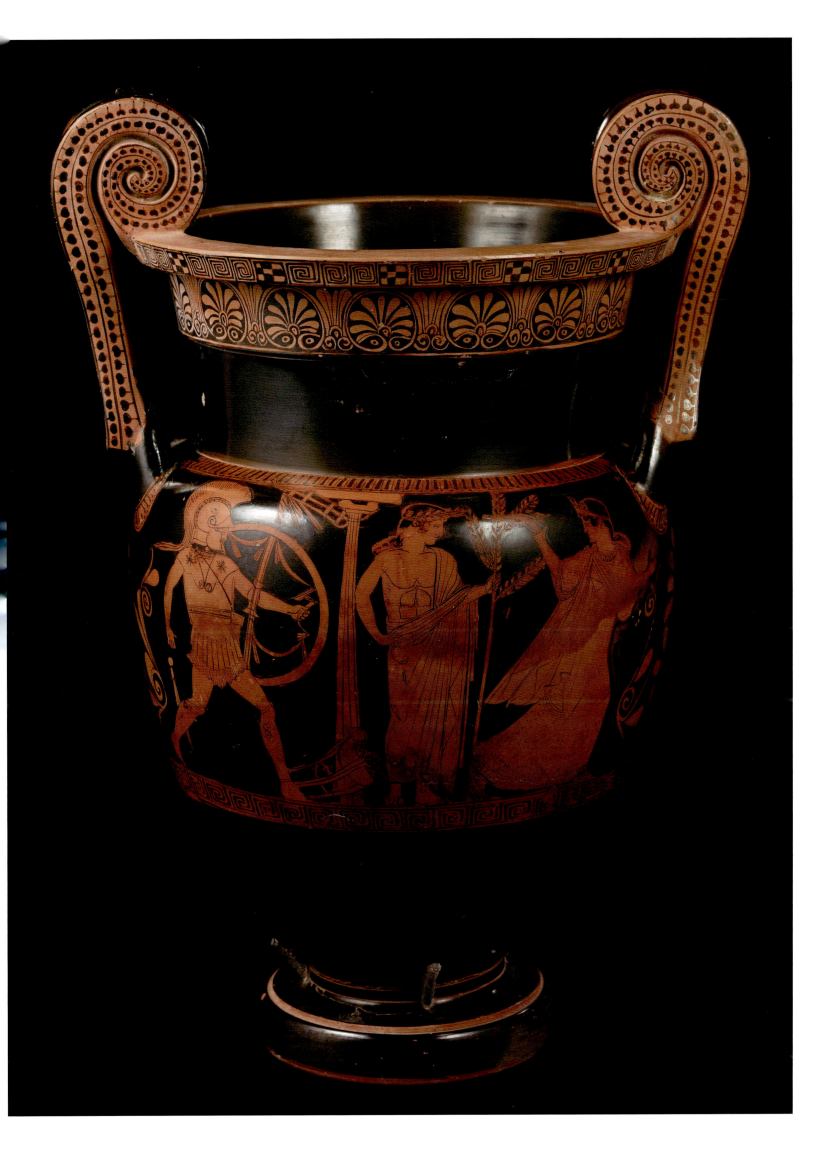

陶质年轻竖琴手或缪斯像

公元前 3 世纪

西吉斯蒙多－卡斯特罗梅迪亚诺博物馆藏

Terracotta statue of a young lyre player or Muse

3rd century BCE

Sigismondo Castromediano Museum, Lecce

陶质海厄森斯 – 阿波罗

公元前 3 世纪
塔兰托国家考古博物馆藏

Terracotta statue of Hyakinthos-Apollo

3rd century BCE
National Archaeological Museum of Taranto (MArTA)

卢坎尼亚红绘斟酒壶

公元前 410 – 前 390 年
塔兰托国家考古博物馆藏

Lucanian red-figure oinochoe

410 BCE - 390 BCE
National Archaeological Museum of Taranto (MArTA)

普利亚红绘钟形调酒缸

公元前 400 – 前 375 年
塔兰托国家考古博物馆藏

Apulian red-figure bell krater

400 BCE - 375 BCE
National Archaeological Museum of Taranto (MArTA)

普利亚钟形覆彩调酒缸

公元前 4 世纪
西吉斯蒙多－卡斯特罗梅迪亚诺博物馆藏

Apulian overpainted Polychrome bell krater

4th century BCE
Sigismondo Castromediano Museum, Lecce

普利亚钟形调酒缸

公元前 380 – 前 360 年
西吉斯蒙多 – 卡斯特罗梅迪亚诺博物馆藏

Apulian bell krater

380 BCE - 360 BCE
Sigismondo Castromediano Museum, Lecce

覆彩双耳酒瓶

公元前 300 年

西吉斯蒙多－卡斯特罗梅迪亚诺博物馆藏

Overpainted double-handled wine jug (Pelike)

300 BCE

Sigismondo Castromediano Museum, Lecce

普利亚红绘钟形调酒缸

公元前 370 - 前 350 年
西吉斯蒙多－卡斯特罗梅迪亚诺博物馆藏

Apulian red-figure bell-krater

370 BCE - 350 BCE
Sigismondo Castromediano Museum, Lecce

阿提卡红绘钟形调酒缸

公元前 440 – 前 430 年

西吉斯蒙多 – 卡斯特罗梅迪亚诺博物馆藏

Attic red-figure bell krater

440 BCE - 430 BCE

Sigismondo Castromediano Museum, Lecce

阿提卡白底式油瓶

公元前 500 – 前 490 年
塔兰托国家考古博物馆藏

Attic white-ground lekythos

500 BCE - 490 BCE
National Archaeological Museum of Taranto (MArTA)

阿提卡黑绘深口翘耳杯

公元前 500 年

塔兰托国家考古博物馆藏

Attic black-figure deep-bellied skyphos

500 BCE

National Archaeological Museum of Taranto (MArTA)

普利亚红绘深口平耳杯

公元前 4 世纪中叶
西吉斯蒙多－卡斯特罗梅迪亚诺博物馆藏

Apulian red-figure skyphos

Mid-4th century BCE
Sigismondo Castromediano Museum, Lecce

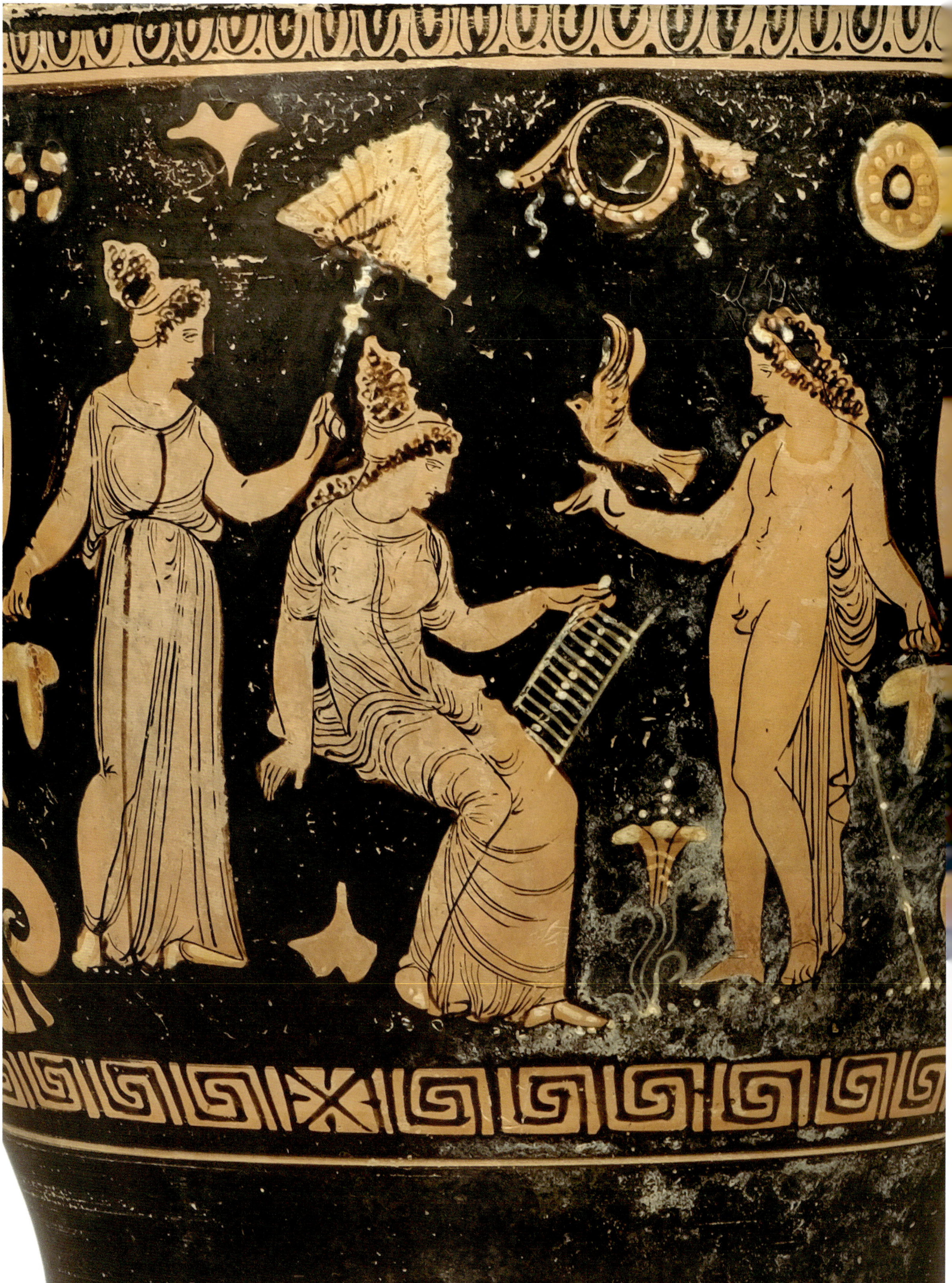

覆彩精油瓶

公元前 3 世纪
塔兰托国家考古博物馆藏

Overpainted Polychrome perfume vase (Alabastron)

3rd century BCE

National Archaeological Museum of Taranto (MArTA)

那提亚式覆彩盆

公元前 320 – 前 300 年
里贝佐布林迪西博物馆藏

Overpainted Polychrome gnathian basin

320 BCE - 300 BCE

Ribezzo Archaeological Museum, Brindisi

覆彩钟形调酒缸

公元前 4 世纪末
西吉斯蒙多 – 卡斯特罗梅迪亚诺博物馆藏

Overpainted Polychrome bell krater

Late 4th century BCE
Sigismondo Castromediano Museum, Lecce

带环铜钹

公元前 1 世纪
塔兰托国家考古博物馆藏

Copper cymbals with rings (Kymbala)

1st century BCE
National Archaeological Museum Taranto (MArTA)

普利亚覆彩弧形瓶

公元前 3 世纪下半叶

西吉斯蒙多－卡斯特罗梅迪亚诺博物馆藏

Apulian overpainted flask (Bombylios)

Second half of the 3rd century BCE

Sigismondo Castromediano Museum, Lecce

赫拉克勒斯

希腊英雄、育种、移牧

Herakles

GREEK HERO, BREEDING, AND TRANSHUMANCE

大力神赫拉克勒斯是古希腊神话传说中最伟大的英雄。传说赫拉憎恶他，让他发疯并杀了自己的妻儿。为此，他要完成十二项艰巨任务来救赎自己。人们喜爱这位半人半神的英雄，很大一部分是认同他克服一切困难的非凡事迹和坚忍不拔的高尚人品。

Herakles, the mighty hero, is considered the greatest hero in Greek mythological legends. The story goes that Hera despised him and made him go mad, leading him to kill his own wife and children. As a result, he had to complete twelve challenging labors to atone for his actions. People admire this demigod hero, largely due to his extraordinary feats of overcoming obstacles and his unwavering noble character.

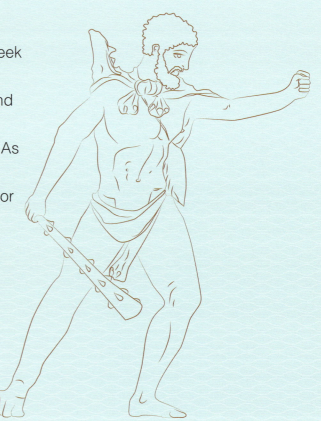

赫拉克勒斯头像单把角杯

公元前 330 – 前 310 年

雅达博物馆藏

Mono-handled rhyton in the shape of the head of Herakles

330 BCE - 310 BCE

Jatta National Archaeological Museum, Ruvo di Puglia

赫拉克勒斯铜像

公元前 3 世纪 – 前 1 世纪
西吉斯蒙多 – 卡斯特罗梅迪亚诺博物馆藏

Bronze statuette of Herakles

3rd century BCE - 1st century BCE
Sigismondo Castromediano Museum, Lecce

赫拉克勒斯雕像

公元 2 世纪 – 3 世纪
福贾市民博物馆藏

Herakles statue

2nd century CE - 3rd century CE
Civic Museum of Foggia

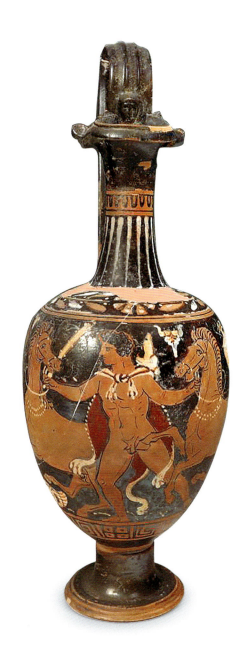

普利亚红绘斟酒壶

公元前 340 – 前 320 年
卡诺萨国家考古博物馆藏

Apulian red-figure oinochoe

340 BCE - 320 BCE
National Archaeological Museum of Canosa

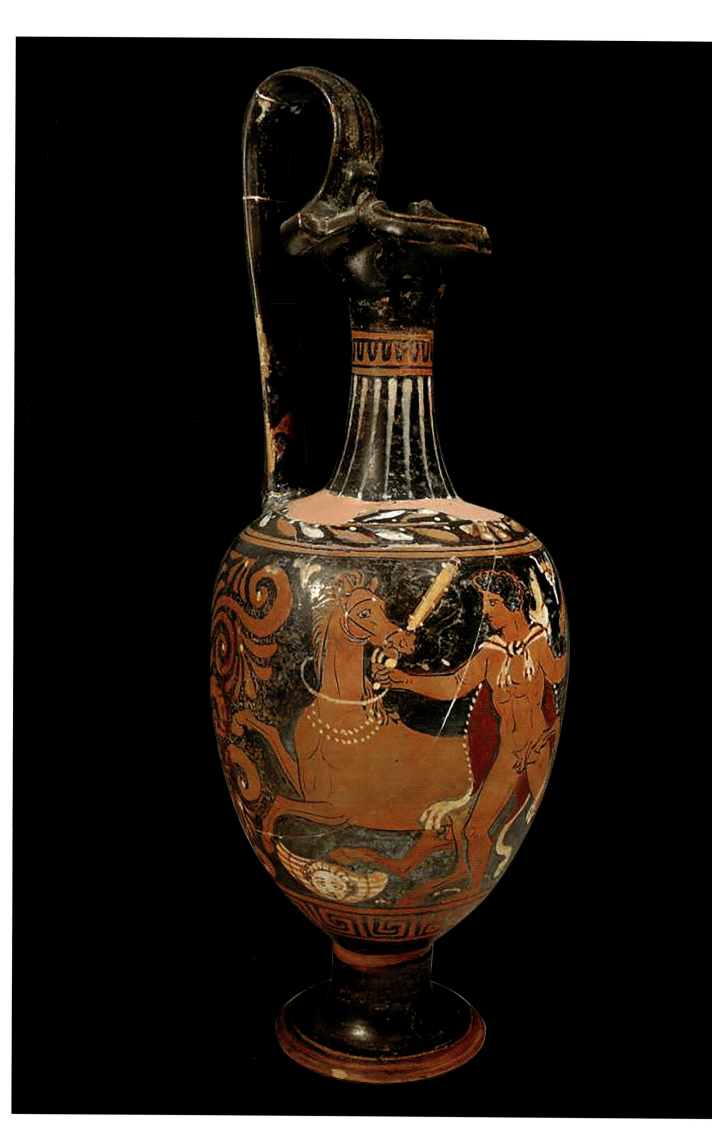

梅萨皮亚蝶饰壶

公元前 5 世纪上半叶
西吉斯蒙多－卡斯特罗梅迪亚诺博物馆藏

Messapian trozzella (Decorated jug)

Second half of the 5th century BCE
Sigismondo Castromediano Museum, Lecce

普利亚红绘钟形调酒缸

公元前 425 – 前 400 年

雅达博物馆藏

Apulian red-figure bell krater

425 BCE - 400 BCE

Jatta National Archaeological Museum, Ruvo di Puglia

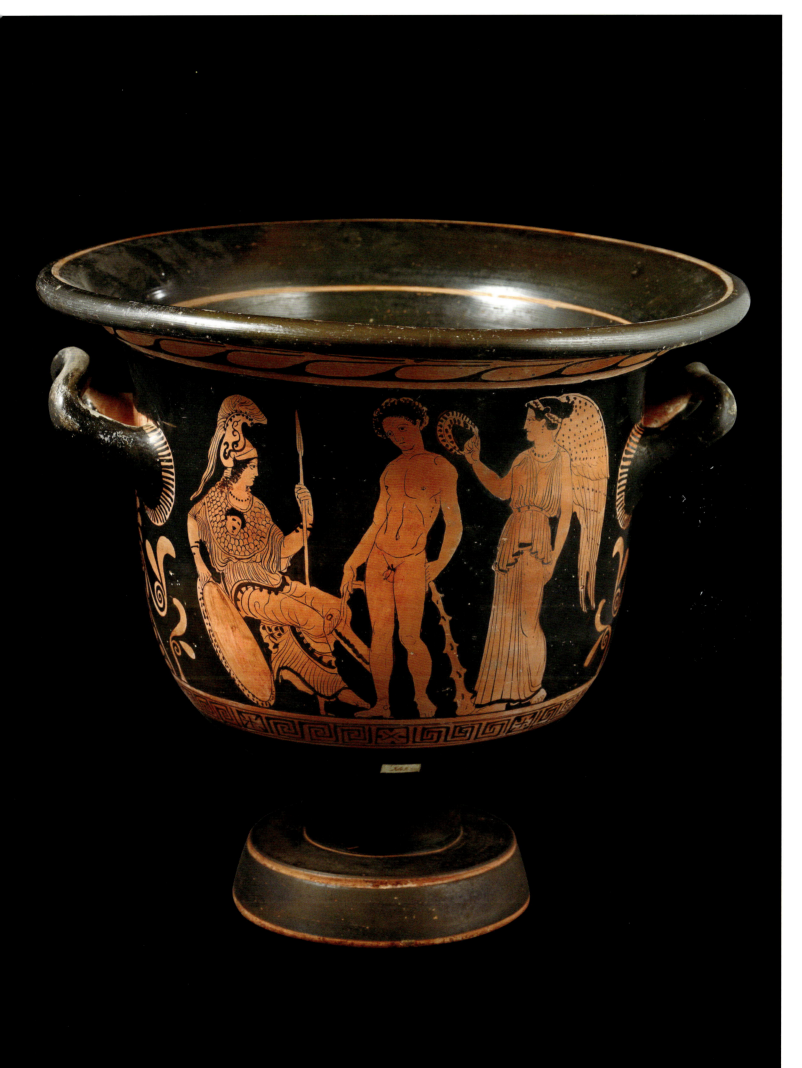

阿提卡红绘双耳水罐

公元前 4 世纪早期

塔兰托国家考古博物馆藏

Attic red-figure hydria

Early 4th century BCE

National Archaeological Museum of Taranto (MArTA)

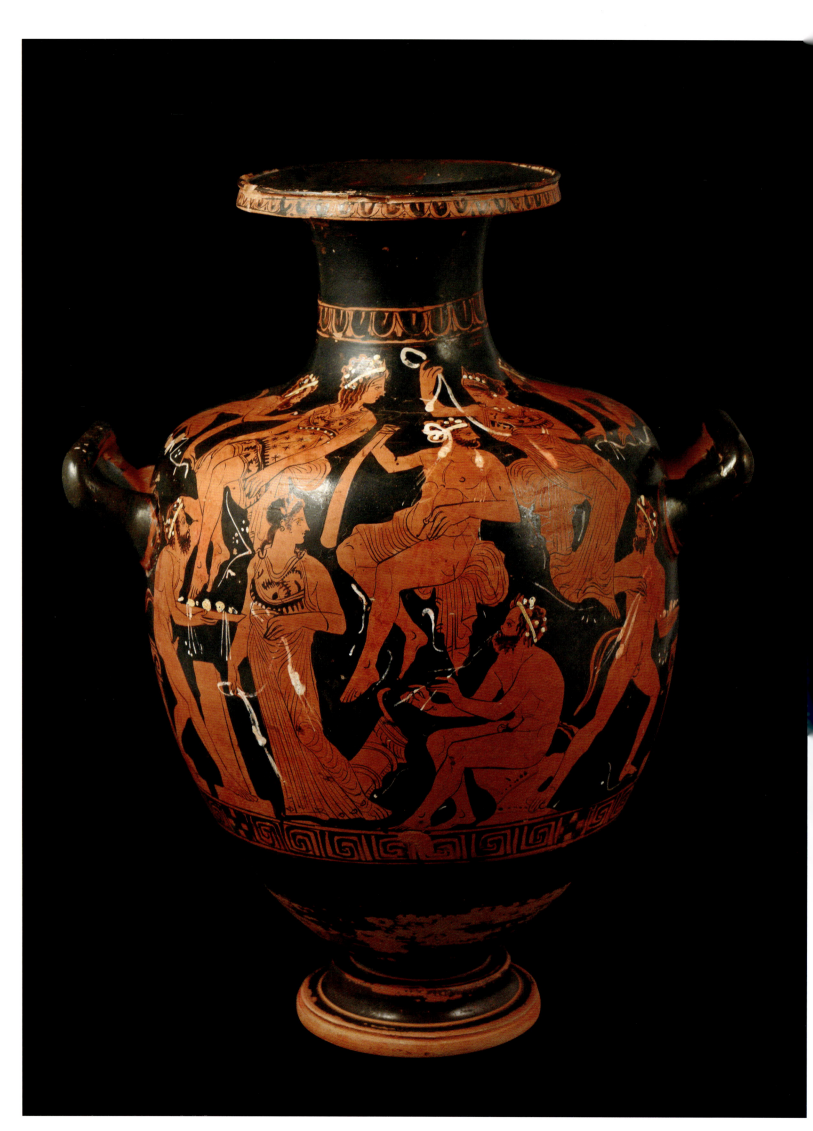

普利亚红绘钟形调酒缸

公元前 420 – 前 400 年

西吉斯蒙多 – 卡斯特罗梅迪亚诺博物馆藏

Apulian red-figure bell krater

420 BCE - 400 BCE

Sigismondo Castromediano Museum, Lecce

普利亚红绘蜷耳调酒缸

公元前 4 世纪

阿尔塔穆拉国家考古博物馆藏

Apulian red-figure volute krater

4th century BCE

National Archaeological Museum of Altamura

2

意大利艺术家数字沉浸式艺术

Digital and Immersive Art Exhibition of Italian Artists

从过去到未来

From the Past to the Future

阿莱西娅·罗洛
Alessia Rollo

阿莱西娅·罗洛是意大利著名摄影与合成艺术的女艺术家，专注于亚得里亚海的文化传统，通过对比和对主题的深入理解，为研究人类与自然提供新的观点。

Field A1 是阿莱西娅·罗洛视觉作品的制作团队。

Alessia Rollo is a famous Italian female artist in photography and synthetic art. She focuses on the cultural traditions of the Adriatic Sea and provides new perspectives for the study of humanity and nature by comparison and in-depth understanding of themes.

Field A1 is the curatorial team of Alessia Rollo's visual artworks on display at the exhibition.

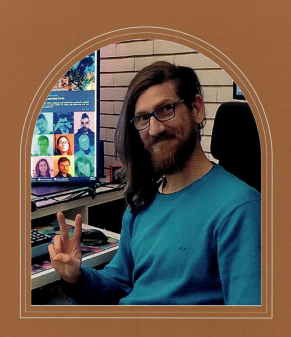

罗伯特·桑托罗
Roberto Santoro

罗伯特·桑托罗是意大利著名数字艺术家，意大利新兴科技艺术的领军人物。2014 年，创新性将 3D 设计应用于舞台剧、芭蕾和时装秀。

Roberto Santoro is a well-known Italian digital artist and a leading figure representing art of emerging technology in Italy. In 2014，he innovatively applied 3D designs to stage dramas, ballets and fashion shows.

Work Creator：Roberto Santoro	作品创作：罗伯特·桑托罗
Choreographer：Vito Cassano	舞蹈编制：维托·卡萨诺
Dancers：Francesco Lacatena/ Grazia Micoli	舞蹈：佛兰切斯科·拉卡提娜 / 格拉夏·米科莉
Music Creator：Kyotolp/ Rome in Reverse	音乐创作：科托 / 颠倒罗马
Special Supporter：Locorotondo Council	特别支持：洛科罗东多市政厅
Mirror House Design Creativity	镜屋设计创意

镜屋

创意设计

Mirror house

DESIGN CREATIVITY

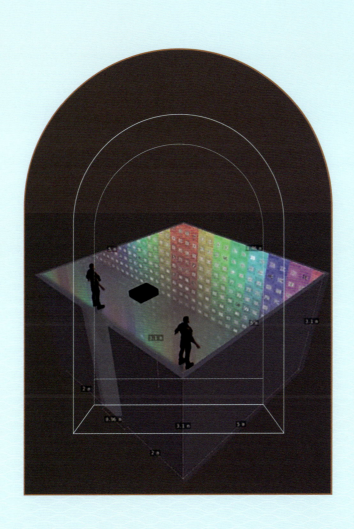

创意设计

Mirror house

DESIGN CREATIVITY

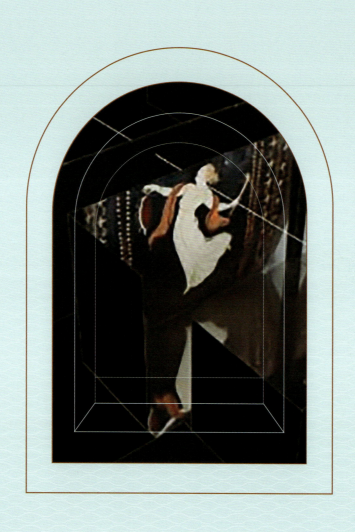

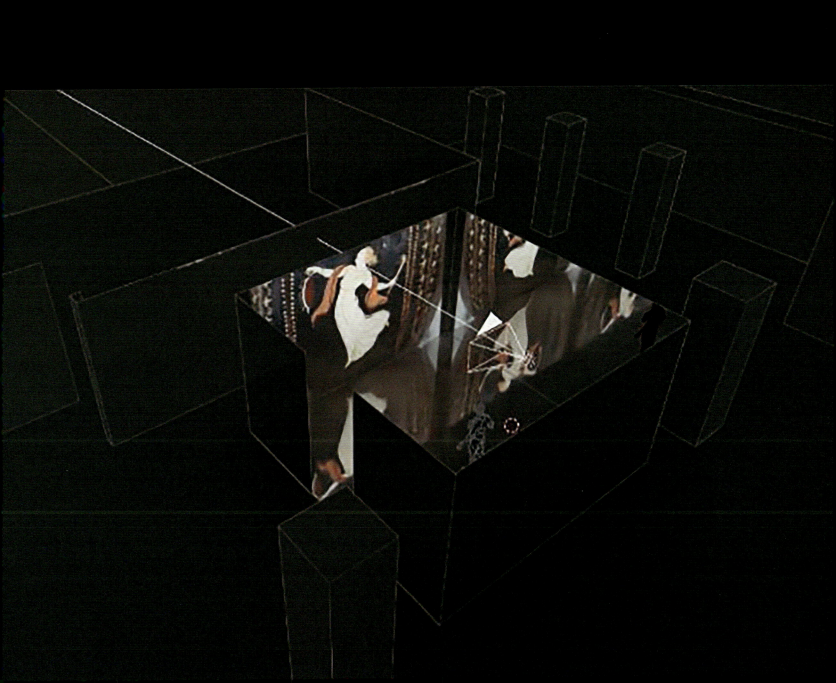

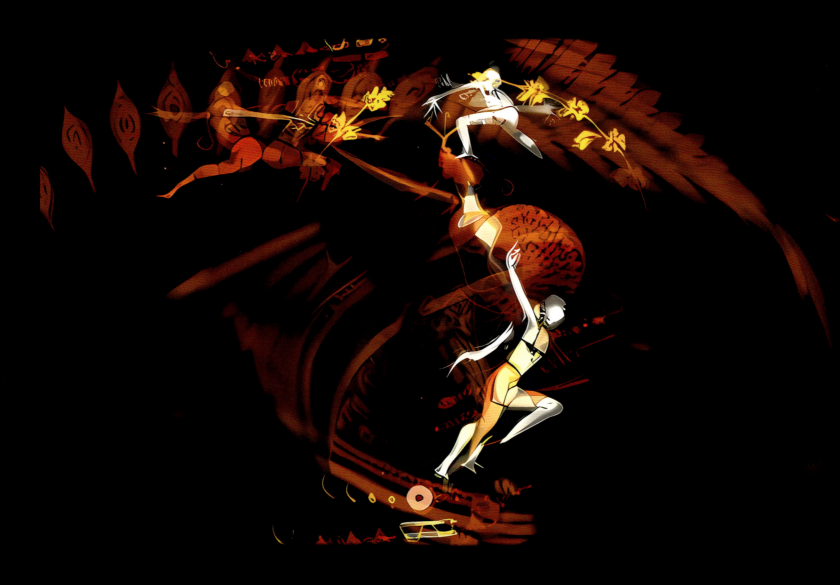

3

Art and Culture of Puglia

普利亚艺术文化

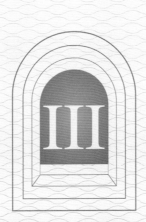

永恒的绚美
Eternal Beauty

展厅

现场照片墙

Exhibition

HALL SITE PHOTO WALL

普利亚

文化遗产和自然风光图片展示

Apulia

PICTURES OF PUGLIA'S CULTURAL HERITAGE AND NATURAL SCENERY

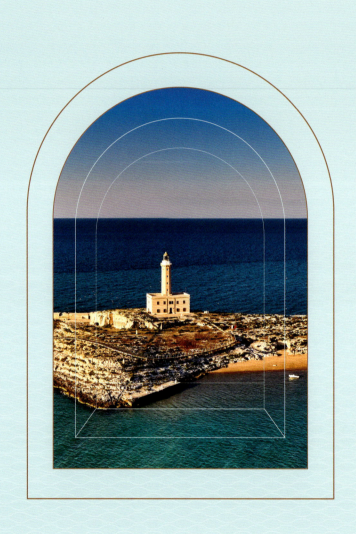

普利亚的古城

Andrea Pistolesi 版权摄影家授权

Ancient City of Puglia

Licensed by Andrea Pistolesi Copyright Photographer

普利亚北部海滨古城 Vieste

Andrea Pistolesi 版权摄影家授权

The old seaside town of Vieste in northern Puglia

Licensed by Andrea Pistolesi Copyright Photographer

世界非物质文化遗产胜地 POLIGNANO A MARE

Richard James Taylor 版权摄影家授权

■

World Intangible Cultural Heritage Resorts POLIGNANO A MARE

Licensed by Richard James Taylor Copyright Photographer

普利亚的海

The Sea of Puglia

普利亚圣佛卡

San Foc of Puglia

Locorotondo 市的葡萄梯田

Regione Puglia 普利亚大区政府授权

Grape terraces in Locorotondo Municipality

Licensed by Regione Puglia Copyright Photographer

普利亚中部 Trani 市的海边教堂

Antonio e Roberto Tartagliene 版权摄影家授权

Church by the Sea in Trani, Central Puglia

Licensed by Antonio e Roberto Tartagliene Copyright Photographer

美国国家地理杂志评选的世界前 3 最美自然景观之地：普利亚北部 Gargano 自然保护区

Mimmo Attademo 版权摄影家授权

National Geographic's TOP 3 Most Beautiful Natural Places in the World: Gargano Nature Reserve, Northern Puglia

Licensed by Mimmo Attademo Copyright Photographer

普利亚北部 Vieste，Gargano 自然保护区

Mimmo Attademo 版权摄影家授权

North of Puglia Vieste, Gargano Nature Reserve

Licensed by Mimmo Attademo Copyright Photographer

Ostuni 与 Fasano 的橄榄树林

Regione Puglia 普利亚大区政府授权

Olive groves in Ostuni and Fasano

Licensed by Regione Puglia Copyright Photographer

千年橄榄树

Leonardo D'Angelo 版权摄影家授权

Millennium Olive Tree

Licensed by Leonardo D'Angelo Copyright Photographer

Polignano 古城天然悬崖浴场（这里是每年举办世界悬崖高台跳水的地方）

The natural cliff baths of the old town of Polignano (This is where the world's cliff high dive is held each year)

Santa Cesarea Terme 的峻峭岩石

Mimmo e Giacomo Guglielmi 版权摄影家授权

High and steep rocks of Santa Cesarea Terme

Licensed by Mimmo e Giacomo Guglielmi Copyright Photographer

巴里市海边渔港

Franco Cappellari 版权摄影家授权

Seaside Fishing Harbor, Bari

Licensed by Franco Cappellari Copyright Photographer

正在准备嘉年华的舞蹈家们

Dancers preparing for Carnival

普利亚特色 Taranta 嘉年华

Puglia Features Taranta Carnival

日间的嘉年华舞蹈

Daytime Carnival Dances

拥有"世界最好面包品牌"的城市——Altamura 市

■

The city with the "best bread brand in the world" - Altamura

Alberobello 圆顶小屋

Alberobello Dome Cottage

Alberobello 的圆顶小屋与橄榄树

Regione Puglia 普利亚大区政府授权

Alberobello Dome Cottage and olive tree

Licensed by Regione Puglia Copyright Photographer

Castel del Monte 城堡

Castel del Monte castles

普利亚 Otranto 市的教堂

Franco Cappellari 版权摄影家授权

Church in Otranto, Puglia

Licensed by Franco Cappellari Copyright Photographer

欧洲最早的巴洛克城市莱切 Lecce 中心的广场

CE Bevilacqua 版权摄影家授权

Europe's first Baroque city, Lecce Center Square

Licensed by CE Bevilacqua Copyright Photographer

圣诞老人诞生的"巴里市的 Bari,Cattedrale 教堂"

Antonio e Roberto Tartaglione 版权摄影家授权

The church where Santa Claus was born - Cattedrale Church, Bari.

Licensed by Antonio e Roberto Tartaglione Copyright Photographer

最小的悬崖教堂 Ceglie Messapica

Mimmo e Giacomo Guglielmi 版权摄影家授权

Smallest Cliff Church Ceglie Messapica

Licensed by Mimmo e Giacomo Guglielmi Copyright Photographer

Canne della Battaglia, Barletta 巴列塔的考古遗址

Archaeological sites in Barletta

巴里市古代通往罗马的路标 Bari，chiesa Bizantina

Ancient signposts to Rome in the city of Bari chiesa Bizantina

结 语
Conclusion

History is bygone, but splendor and beauty are eternal.

The Western civilization traces its roots back to remote antiquity, and Puglia is a key place to breed, germinate and grow this civilization.

Today, Puglia is still the first gateway for resources of the Middle East and the Balkan Peninsula to access to Europe. Taranto Port is still a key hub of trade and culture between the East and the West.

Puglia is awarded one of the Ten Most Beautiful Places of the World by National Geographic and is the most popular holiday destination in Europe. Here you can enjoy both natural sceneries and cultural roots and atmosphere nurtured by the culture and history of ancient Greece over thousands of years.

The Land of the Gods. The Spirit of the Life.

历史如水而流逝，绚丽与唯美依旧。

如果说，西方文明源远流长，普利亚就是文明之种孕育、发芽、不断壮大的关键之地……

今日的普利亚，仍是中东和巴尔干半岛资源进入欧洲的第一门户，塔兰托港仍然是东西方贸易和文化的重要枢纽。

今日的普利亚，被美国国家地理杂志评为世界十大最美区域之一，是欧洲最热门的度假胜地。这里有自然风光，更有数千年古希腊历史沉淀造就的独一无二的文化根基与氛围。

众神之地，唯美丰硕，源远流长……

效果图

Pesentation Of Formal

DESIGN DRAWINGS

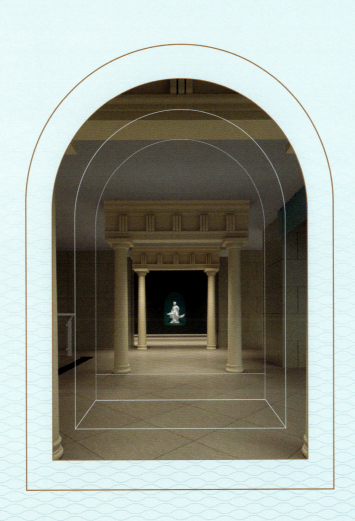

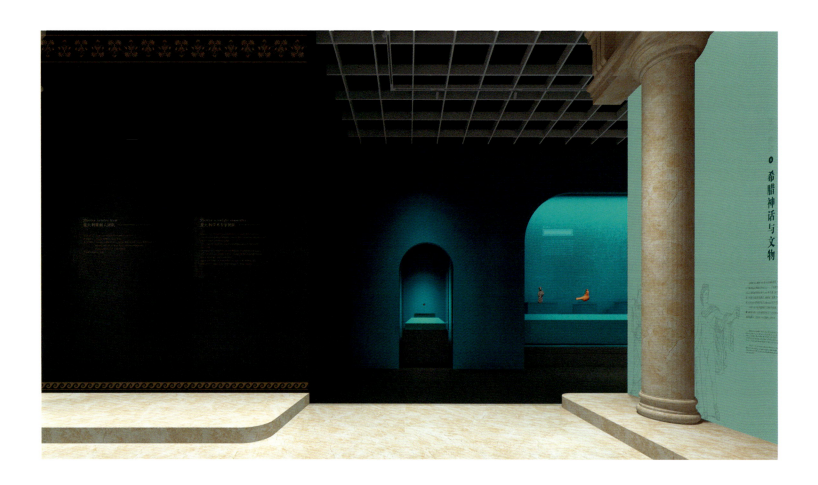

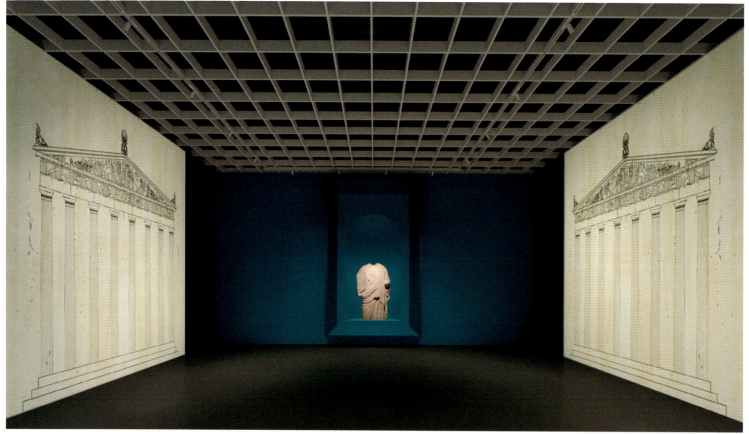

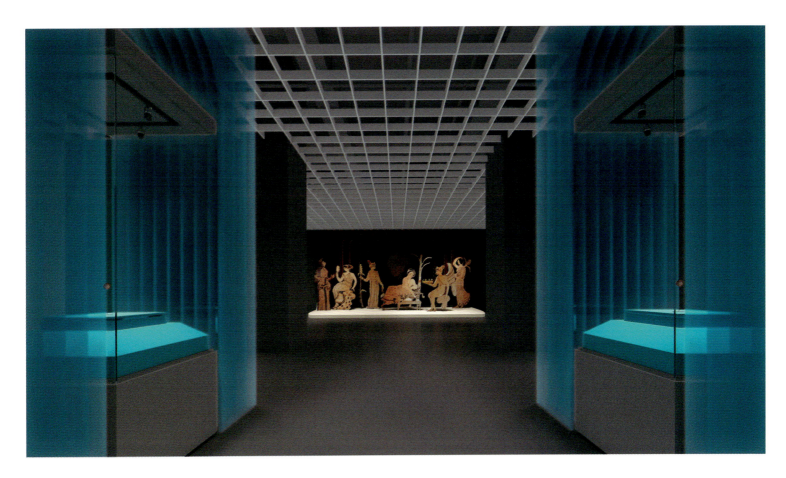

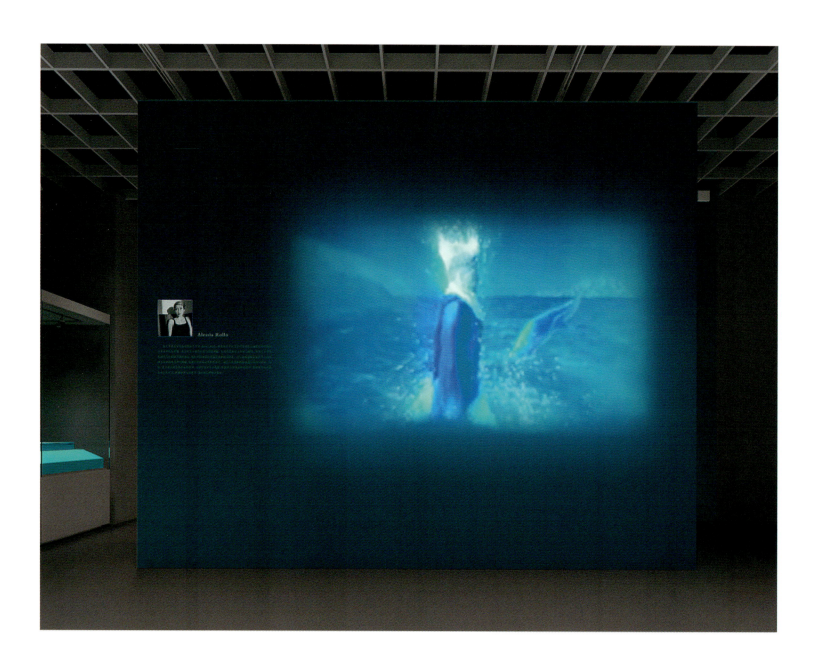

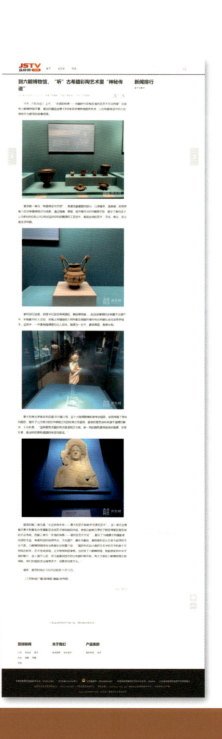

七彩的夏日 走进六朝博物馆 真切感受古希腊文明

海仙女乘坐"鱼尾马人"陶塑像

它们漂洋过海而来

这个盛夏来六朝博物馆
感受古希腊"永恒的绚美"

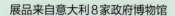

展品来自意大利8家政府博物馆

据悉,本次展览由南京市博物总馆、中国文物交流中心、意大利普利亚政府主办,六朝博物馆承办,意大利8家政府博物馆提供藏品支持。展览以古希腊神话中的六位神祇作为组织展品的故事线索,通过陶器、雕塑、钱币等精美文物,呈现普利亚地区于公元前6世纪至公元2世纪,800年间精湛的工艺技术与人们丰富的生活风貌和心灵生活。

走进展厅,来到"希腊神话与文物"单元,古希腊的风情和韵味扑面而来。波塞冬、得墨忒耳、雅典娜、狄俄尼索斯、阿波罗、赫拉克勒斯六位古希腊神话中神祇的故事,在一件件精美的文物上如画卷般展现在观众眼前。在这些璀璨的古希腊文化遗产中,彩陶最为引人注目,彩陶上所描绘的人物形象及周围环境均与古希腊社会生活息息相关。

以古希腊神话中神祇为布展线索

对于意大利南部居民而言,海洋既神秘又富饶。海豚骑手塔拉斯陶俑、普利亚式红绘双耳酒瓶、海仙女乘坐"鱼尾马人"陶塑像、普利亚红绘女妖斯库拉角杯……此次展示出的瓶画、雕塑等珍贵文物融合了神话与现实,展现出独特的海洋印象。

雅典娜是古希腊神话中的战争女神、智慧女神。和雅典娜相关的展品有阿提卡白底

紫袍陶俑

式油瓶、铜质油灯、普利亚红绘尊形调酒瓶、卢坎尼亚红绘调酒瓶、猫头鹰图像双耳杯等。

展品中还有很多精美的红绘酒瓶,它们相对应的是古希腊神话中的酒神和狂欢之神狄俄尼索斯。狄俄尼索斯位列奥林匹斯十二主神之一的神祇,这里的展品大多跟酒神神话、狂欢节相关。阿波罗是古希腊神话中的光明之神、音乐之神、预言之神和医疗之神。其标志性乐器是竖琴,阿提卡黑绘油瓶、覆彩精油瓶等文物都在讲述他的故事。

油灯是古代常见的器皿,给古代生活的漫漫长夜带来珍贵的光明,展品中一些瓶画中描绘的人物常手持装有橄榄油的油瓶。早期油灯为陶土或石制的盘子,之后使用的材料有青铜、金、银和玻璃。

在盛夏里感受到宁静的力量

展厅中央的一件阿提卡黑绘油瓶,极为精美。瓶身图案为阿波罗弹奏七弦琴的场景。几匹骏马拉着的战车后面,身穿白色长袍的阿波罗全神贯注地弹奏着竖琴。

沉静典雅的紫袍陶俑,虽然小巧,却吸引了现场观众齐刷刷的目光。陶俑女子身穿紧身上衣和一件包裹身体直到小腿的斗篷,斗篷颜色从粉红色,紫色到淡紫色过渡,色彩独特,造型优美,在南京炎热的盛夏里,看着它能感受到一种宁静的力量。

此外,展览第二单元为"从过去到未来——意大利艺术家数码及沉浸艺术展",主要展示意大利著名女性摄影及合成艺术家Alessia Rollo的数码作品,以及意大利知名数码艺术家Roberto Santoro的IFINI-TY ROOM装置,使观众沉浸式了解亚得里亚海区域的文化传统。展览第三单元为"永恒的绚美——普利亚艺术文化",展示了30幅意大利摄影家的授权作品,内容包括普利亚自然风光、文化遗产、嘉年华景观,展现普利亚从古至今延续的文化气息。

"中欧虽相隔万里,但海洋和高山没有阻隔我们交往的脚步。南京市博物总馆党委书记、馆长许强表示,"在欧洲文化史上,意大利普利亚是古希腊文明向古罗马文明过渡的发源地,既充满醇厚的文化底蕴,也充满自然的韵味。感谢意大利方对本次展览的支持,让璀璨的古希腊文化遗产漂洋过海而来。"

南京晨报/爱南京记者 刘静 摄影报道

LIVE 零距离　暑假，来看希腊时代彩陶特展
7月27日（生）成品油价格26日24时上调，调整后，江…
暑假、来看希腊时代彩陶特展

35万人次观展！"永恒的纯美"特展在南京博物院

永恒的纯美
南京站展览闭幕分享会

南京日报　学习贯彻党的二十大精神

古希腊瑰宝陶展示"永恒的纯美"

江苏城市　荔枝新闻　微博视频号 @荔枝新闻

LIVE 零距离　（暑期期间）小朋友比较多
8月14日　[民生]今年上半年，全国新…

今日起至10月8日
六朝博物馆取消"周一闭馆"

迎接 超级黄金周　国庆　A4　南京日报

南京城，靓了
红红火火！国旗中国结 高高挂起来

花团锦簇！满城花如海 节日氛围浓

9月29日—10月6日 16时至22时
夫子庙景区欲准入

"文化大餐"已熬好，展馆活动精彩多
在博物馆，遇见美好生活

迎中秋 猜灯谜

高速公路日均出口流量预计明比增长超四成

江岸水幕秀
点亮夜空

LIVE 这个七夕 有一份专属博物馆的浪漫

既是意大利
何来古希腊

普利亚是意大利南部的一个大区，与希腊隔海相望。那时文化发展史上也是古希腊文化与本土文化的文明世界。希腊这种陶瓷器技艺在这片土地中那样深，深入人们生活诸多角落。

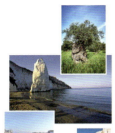

当地人用白门口瓷陶传的欢乐和彩绘记录生活，讲述情感。这些日常瓷陶艺人用白陶瓷上，陶耕地，用力量，编绘成台。

如今，在六朝博物馆看到中国，在六朝博物馆运行六的中国观众诉说文明的故事。

永恒的绚美
希腊时代彩陶及普利亚艺术文化特展

简述中，一件件文物影一件件绚丽，并借这子立体的的文物影，唱陶器、绘陶大，唱组大、组助各的故事呈在艺术的网间奔映。

永恒的绚美
希腊时代彩陶及
普利亚艺术文化特展
THE ART OF THE PAST

07 26
11 12

陶瓷的雕塑，故事，技艺....与水什（星）希腊亚希腊呈展现的出由者文物为你讲这希腊种讲述的传说故事，六朝博物馆这陶呈与希腊文物与意大利亚两版的年展味诸"陶诸"、次由真白，还有一公六朝呈更大的布展艺文家的戏着方式现？

NOVA

Cina: al via mostra su cultura italiana a Nanchino

Nanchino, 27 aug 14:48 - (AGENZIA) - Una mostra sulla civiltà antica, l'arte moderna e la cultura della regione italiana della Puglia ha preso il via in la provincia orientale cinese

来六朝博物馆馆解锁地中海风情

展览单元简介

第一单元

公元古希腊神话为故事，通过精美文物展开普利亚十公司和9世纪新公元八世纪800年描述的工艺技术与古六朝本墨的心灵生活，六位神物诉说像

陶罐之种

千年一脉，兰制之花颜间诸绝、传那的文化记忆融于众里融入现代生活之中，崇拉瓦展式空间Infinity Room装置，由意大利艺术家罗Roberto Santoro创作，文物影，呈现主题，永过古现时单线。

第二单元

意大利是光洲亚两希之辉的国度。本单元八大力美展的诸普利亚十七世纪，诸陶的艺术文化的...千年以来，古六大力美文化记忆诸呈现。

酒神，狂欢之神

出群之神，音乐之神

大力神

沉浸式观展艺术影与数化生活数字分像化艺术作品本Alessia Aoto化影陶化像，公司意大利和高的和科技不展Roberto Santoro的Infinity Room装置，现么可了解由有像文化化的由这种数化艺术体现先。

第三单元 永恒的绚美——
意大利艺术文化

普利亚作为古希腊陶的最佳诸陶在诸方之一，是古希腊文明的文明化语变诸界诸，这是陶有本普这古希腊文化诸传。

普利亚诸盎然风光，文化遗产，诸陶诸中诸诸...30余描普大利诸陶诸诸陶的诸的的作品展现了诸利回诸与古六朝诸诸时代的问题。

展览美图欣赏
Museum beauty pictures for

打开有有种文化的魅力，跟中诸古千年许习诸六的诸像，这下展示来六朝博物馆，一场诸诸解诸诸诸诸的中海风情，诸诸诸诸诸六朝诸文明。

批判"不见之美，

这个六诸诸诸诸诸诸诸...文明古诸之诸的诸诸诸诸古诸的诸诸诸。诸千的诸诸诸诸诸诸诸诸诸诸诸诸诸诸诸诸诸诸诸诸诸诸诸诸。

回溯古希腊，对西方人来说是一种循环，对我们而言，是一种溯源的思念。"永恒的旋律——希腊时代彩陶及普利亚艺术文化珍藏"让您穿越追寻真实，地中海将或文明之风就这样改写了长江的这头。

绚美 文化

欧洲文化史上，普利亚是古希腊文明向古罗马文明过渡的发源地。

公元前8世纪起，希腊人在此建立殖民地，带来文化技术的传播。时至今日，普利亚仍保有多处古希腊文化遗产，宛若一颗颗散落人间的珍宝遗珠。

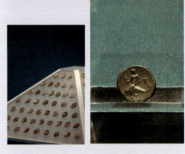

沿着多立克柱式走廊深入此展厅，古希腊六位神祇的故事在这里徐徐展开，普利亚的展馆将空间不规则地分隔，层次丰富的陈展令观众穿梭其中，如探秘途中邂逅一幕幕不期而遇。

展陈设计不仅是为还原古希腊文明之美，还衡量信息与细节的传达。光影聚焦文物，观众与展品产生情感共鸣。

现场还计对视障观众特别设立可触摸展品体验区，文物3D模型及复制品介绍拓展了展览的受众

展览以六位希腊神祇为事新展开，再现了古希腊神话传说中对人民生活的影响，通过动漫、帧作及现代工艺，传递独特的文化魅力。

"地中海风情"

普利亚文化遗存于四世纪，和遭受古希腊传说的影响力，感应博物馆收藏。

"跨时空榴盒"

神秘奇谲诡的海洋激发了人们无穷无尽的创作灵感。公元前400年左右，古希腊人开始在盘子上绘制各种鱼类图案，并用这些特别的盘子盛放美食，现代学者称之为鱼盘。

语述中"海洋与盛宴"单元呈现的这些鱼盘凸显了古希腊人与海洋的不解之缘。古希腊人在鱼盘上绘制盘绘、杯及饰盘食等，盘口边缘凸起以防盛放和享盛时的汁液，便其更具实用性和艺术美感。鱼盘中央回陷部分或用于盛放调味料，或为收集食物汁液所用。

这件公元前580-570年的线口杯，内壁绘制缠绕排列的鱼类及海藻，颜色富于变化，细节刻画精细巧妙。

晚餐 生活是苦，有暇就歇

古希腊人冒为晚餐是一天中最重要的一餐，他们在一天劳作结束时常在餐桌上花去很长时间，同围晚餐吃得相当丰富。

古希腊人喜食烧肉等，展览中这件金属锅便为享煮肉类时使用。其他如火盆、铲子、整烤架、叉子等金属质地的器具在这时份一一应俱全。

吃完正餐，古希腊人会以蜂蜜先加腌味先清浸在的葡和无花果等食粮上，制成传统的"古希腊蜜饼"。此外，梨、石榴、苹果、无花果、坚果、橄榄和李子等水果也倍受欢迎。古希腊人认为石榴等有缠生的象征意义，因此其某与婚盛礼及其底碎仪式相关。

调味剂 嫩柢，真"治"你的

无论是清煮肉类、蔬菜还是烤制面点，古希腊人都会倾向于用橄榄油调味。受古希腊文化影响，普利亚省都普遍使用橄榄油的传统，成干上万株橄榄树种在普利亚省的海岸线上，构成一道道绿色的风景线。展览展示有绵延千年橄榄树的照片，仿佛讲诉着遥远而动人的故事。

更多人说

配合展览、六朝博物馆还推出各类社教活动，包括线下课程《神话里的古希腊·诸神图鉴》及线上课程《妙谈神话》等。推出成人、少儿和亲子版公益学习单，与大众书局联合研发研学课程、少儿文博推广达人"朋朋哥哥"为25组亲子家庭做公益讲座……丰富的展览配套活动让观众领略到文物之美。

少儿参加《神话里的古希腊·诸神图鉴》线下课程

自开展以来，特展相关新闻报道、官方微信微博的浏览量达1522.2万次。《中国日报》、搜狐网等多家网媒和客户端借助华为鸿蒙系统元服务功能推送展讯累计曝光率达4000万次。

预热期、曝光期、持续推广期……不同阶段为宣传把握节奏，让展览持续升温、扩大了展览的影响力和美誉度。

Exhibition promotional poster

DRAFTING DESIGN

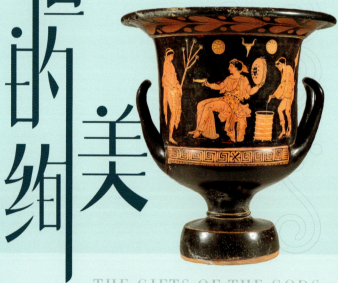

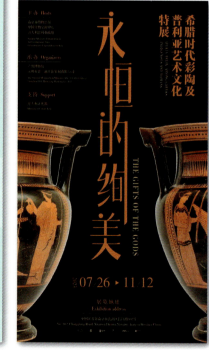

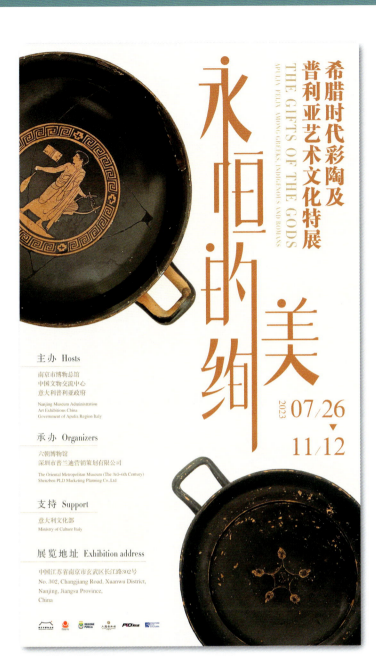
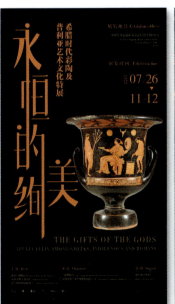

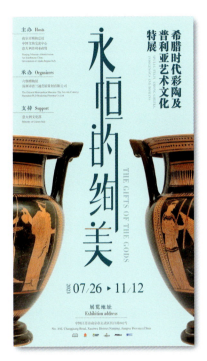
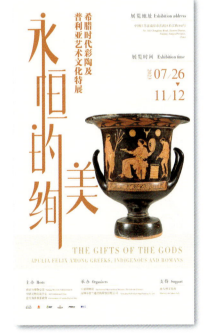

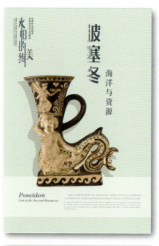

波塞冬
海洋与资源

Poseidon
God of the Sea and Resources

德墨忒耳
粮食与丰饶

Demeter
Grain and Abundance

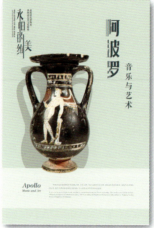

阿波罗
音乐与艺术

Apollo
Music and Art

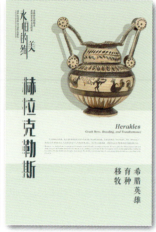

赫拉克勒斯
希腊英雄
育种
移牧

Herakles
Greek Hero, Breeding and Transformation

雅典娜
橄榄树
橄榄油
手工艺

Athena
Olive Tree, Olive Oil, and Crafts

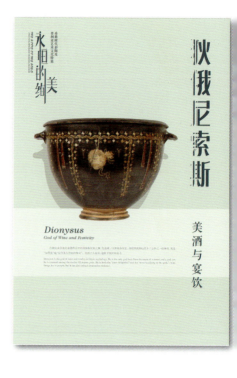

狄俄尼索斯
美酒与宴饮

Dionysus
God of Wine and Festivity

THE GIFTS OF THE GODS

永恒的美

2023
7/26
11/12

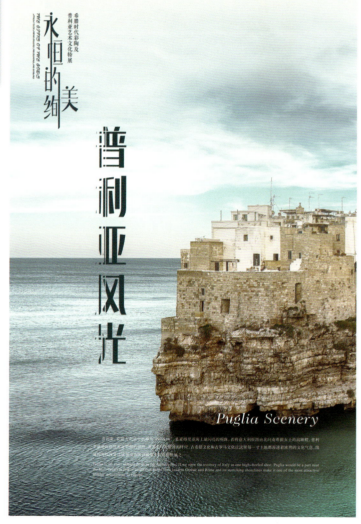

永恒的美

普利亚风光

Puglia Scenery

希腊时代彩陶及普利亚艺术文化特展

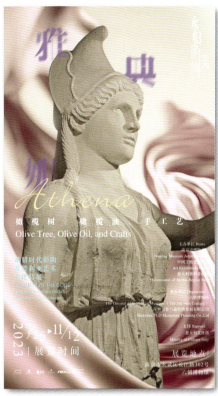

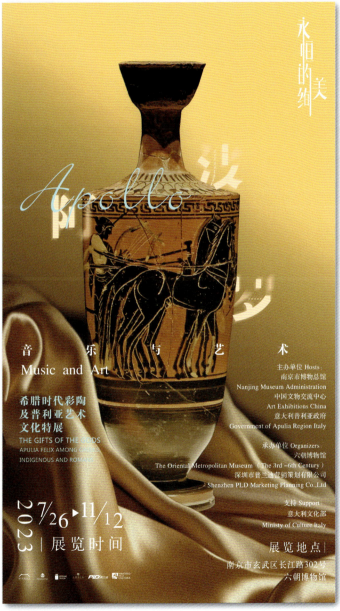

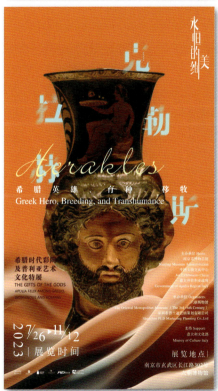

延伸阅读

Extended Reading

The Transmission of Puglia's Cultural Heritage

General Director of Archaeology, Fine Arts and Landscape-Ministry of Culture

Luigi La Rocca

The Apulian territory is witness to a thousand-year history that archaeological documents allow to be reconstructed through a rich and varied fabric of sites and finds belonging to different eras.

The incessant excavation activity carried out by the state structures responsible for the protection of cultural heritage since at least the last quarter of the nineteenth century following the establishment of the Central Directorate of the Excavations and the Museums of the Kingdom entrusted in 1875 to Giuseppe Fiorelli, has allowed the constant interaction between the demands of conservation and the needs of scientific research, which has allowed over time to define and deepen the many themes derived from the analysis of contexts and archaeological documents: the forms of occupation and exploitation of the territory and then the birth and development of settlements in the different geographical and cultural sectors that characterize the region, Daunia, Peucezia, and Messapia; the forms of contact of the alien populations with each other and with the Greek colony of Taranto; the ways and the level of transmission of knowledge and cultures between Greeks and local populations since the archaic era; the effects of the early romanization on the society and the economy of the region from the end of the 4th century BC.

The exhibition The Gifts of the Gods. Apulia Felix among Greeks, indigenous and Romans is an important opportunity to transfer to a people apparently far away for customs and traditions such as China, the picture of a land whose cultural heritage is the result of contacts, exchanges, of interactions between peoples favoured by its intermediate

普利亚文化遗产的传播之路

意大利文化部考古美术及景观局局长
路易吉·拉罗卡

geographical position between East and West of the Mediterranean and that has produced extraordinary archaeological, historical and architectural evidences.

The finds selected by the institutes of the Ministry of Culture, figured ceramics, sculptures, pottery, and objects in metal and terracotta, come in many cases from the main museums of the region; in others, however, the exhibition is the first opportunity for exposure to the public and, therefore, for scientific reinterpretation of contexts found during recent excavations. Visual communication vehicles, but also pages of a book that tell the story of a territory through the testimonies left by the peoples who inhabited it in antiquity.

All this is possible thanks to the accuracy with which the Superintendencies of Archaeology, Fine Arts and Landscape guarantee the protection and the conservation of the archaeological heritage of the Nation, through the excavation activities, the restoration, the study of ancient monuments and finds found, allowing the enhancement, that is, the widest dissemination of knowledge of the cultural heritage and its public use to promote the development of culture.

普利亚大区是千年历史与文献的见证人。考古文献可以通过一系列不同时代丰富的遗址和考古发现得到重建。

随着 1875 年以朱塞佩·菲奥雷利为首的中央考古挖掘局和王国博物馆的成立，由国家文化遗产保护相关机构主持的发掘工作从至少 19 世纪最后的 25 年起，一直在持续有效地进行中，文物保护和科学研究之间的交流也不断深入，许多来源于语境分析和考古文献的主题在时间的推移中得到进一步确认和深化。这些问题包括，占有和剥削领土的不同形式，道尼亚、普乌西蒂亚和梅萨皮亚三个刻画了普利亚地区特征并拥有不同地理、文化的区域中定居点的诞生与发展；不同群体之间的沟通交流及他们与殖民地塔兰托之间的沟通交流及接触情况；自古代以来，希腊人与当地居民之间知识和文化的沟通与传播方式；从公元前 4 世纪末开始，早期罗马化对该地区社会和经济的影响。

举办"永恒的绚美——希腊时代彩陶及普利亚艺术文化特展"是一个非常重要的机会，让普利亚这片土地上的文化遗产，能传播到传统文化与其大相径庭的地方，如中国。得益于它在地中海东西之间的地理位置，这片土地的文化遗产是各民族之间接触、交流和互动的产物，并创造了非凡的考古、历史和建筑景象。

由意大利文化部学术委员会挑选出来的展品，涵盖陶器、雕塑、陶俑、金属和陶土制品。它们来自普利亚大区各个重要博物馆，很多是第一次在公共展览中展出。展览也提供了对近代考古发掘的背景资料重新进行科学解释的机会。本图录也是通过书本的方式，将这片土地上曾居住过的人民留下的历史痕迹进行展示。

之所以能举办此次展览，需要感谢考古、美术和景观管理局监管机构的工作，他们就国家考古遗址进行了精细的保护和保存，组织专业人员对古代文物及古迹进行专业的发掘、修复、研究，并将其广泛地用于公共展览中，使文化遗产得到极大的传播，促进了国家间文化的发展。

Apulia Felix between Past and Future

Director of Department of Tourism Economics of Culture and Enhancement of the Territory-Puglia Region
Aldo Patruno

In 2010, the Puglia Region and the Chinese Province of Guangdong established their first friendly partnership protocol. While the primary focus of the protocol was on areas such as the green economy, SME development, clean energy production from renewable sources, scientific research, and technological innovation, it also included cultural cooperation and promotion of cultural heritage from the perspective of territorial marketing and sustainable tourism, although this was the last area of focus. This protocol marked an important first step in the long journey towards building stable and friendly relations between Puglia and China. However, the path that led to this initial stage was not without its challenges.

Through the exhibition "The Gifts of the Gods: Apulia Felix among Greeks, Indigenous people, and Romans", our region has taken a significant step forward in cultural relations with China. This project represents a shift from mere declarations of intent to the development of a large and ambitious cultural initiative. The exhibition serves as a platform for scientific and cultural cooperation among various institutions involved in research, protection, enhancement, and management of cultural heritage. Rather than just an exhibition, this project is a shared scientific endeavor, not just among Italian partners but also between these partners and Chinese cultural institutions.

Museums are institutions that remain open and connected to current events, registering their impact like seismographs. Therefore, they are contemporary beyond the contents of their collections. The "Gifts of the Gods: Apulia Felix among Greeks, Indigenous people, and Romans" project speaks to the contemporaneity of the ancient, highlighting the relevance

普利亚的富饶丰裕
——从过去到未来

普利亚大区文化旅游与领土部部长
阿尔多·帕特鲁诺

and significance of ancient cultural heritage in the present day.

The original idea for the exhibition was to showcase archaeological Puglia through its extensive history, dating back to the Paleolithic era until the end of the Roman Empire. However, it has now evolved into an international laboratory of cultural proneutrality, representing a concrete example of integration, sharing, and authentic co-design. This project is the result of genuine collaboration between various institutions, including representatives of the Italian State, such as the Regional Directorate of Museums of Puglia, the Regional Secretariat of Puglia, the National Superintendency for the Submerged Cultural Heritage, the three Superintendencies of Archaeology, Fine Arts, and Landscapes of Puglia, the National Archaeological Museum of Taranto, and the Universities of Bari, Foggia, and Salento, as well as Puglia's Department of Tourism, Economy of Culture and Territorial Enhancement. Moreover, the exhibition includes the University of Beijing, ART EXHIBITIONS CHINA, the Nanjing Museum Administration, the Oriental Metropolitan Museum（the 3rd-6th century）, which will host the exhibition, which will host the exhibition, and the network of Puglia's Museums, which provide the archaeological materials that make up the exhibition's narrative.

The exhibition's narrative is conveyed through a carefully curated selection of antiquities, including figurative

早在 2010 年，普利亚大区与中国广东省签订了第一个友好伙伴合作协议，该协议的主要重点是"绿色经济、中小企业发展、可再生能源清洁能源生产、科学研究和技术创新"等领域，同时，也包括文化合作，以及通过从地区营销和可持续性发展的旅游业进行文化遗产的推广。虽然这是最后一个合作领域，但该友好协议标志着普利亚大区与中国在建立稳定友好关系的漫长征程中迈出了重要的第一步。然而，这也是艰难的一步，充满了很多挑战。

通过"永恒的绚美——希腊时代彩陶及普利亚艺术文化特展"，普利亚大区与中国的文化合作关系向前迈出了重要一步。该项目展现了双方从简单的意向声明到文化合作的过程，是双方雄心勃勃的真实合作。此次展览，为意大利与中国的"文化遗产研究与保护，非物质文化遗产研究和运营"等不同文化机构建立了平台，该项目不仅是一个单纯的文化展览展示项目，更是意大利合作伙伴之间及意大利合作机构与中国文化机构之间共同的科研努力。

像地震仪时刻记录地震波一样，博物馆是时刻开放，记录过去并与现在保持紧密联系的机构。因此，它对当代人们思想与生活的影响力，远大于博物馆内藏品所表达的文物内涵。如同此次"永恒的绚美——希腊时代彩陶及普利亚艺术文化特展"项目，讲述古老文物的当代性，强调现在古代文化遗产仍处于重要地位，以及它与当代社会的相关性。

该展览的初衷是展示普利亚大区悠久的考古学历史，讲述从旧石器时代直到罗马帝国末期的历史。然而，此次项目演变成为一个"广泛文化投射性的国际实验室"项目，成为不同团队"整合、共享，协同合作，共同促成"的优秀案例。该项目是各个机构之间真诚合作的结果。意大利方面包括普利亚地区博物馆局、普利亚地区秘书处、国家水下文化遗产监管局、普利亚考古、艺术、景观三个监管局、塔兰托国家考古博物馆、巴里大学、福贾大学和萨伦托大学，以及普利亚旅游、文化经济和领土发展部……中国方面包括北京大学、中国文物交流中心、南京市博物总馆、

ceramics, sculptures, terracotta's, and goldsmiths. These artifacts speak to us about the relationship between the region and the Mediterranean Sea, which has always been a meeting point for various cultures. In ancient times, the agricultural and marine resources of the region nourished the people of Japigi, Messapi, Peuceti, Dauni, and Tarantini, while also inspiring stories and beliefs associated with the profound presence of the Greeks and Romans in the area. The exhibition highlights the central role of wheat and other products of the land, including the vine and olive, as well as music, dance, theater, craftsmanship, and expressions of popular art in the story of Puglia. The region's roots lie in Greek and Roman mythology and history, while its swings stretch towards the future.

主办展览的六朝博物馆……在展览的具体策划执行中，普利亚博物馆体系的专业学者为展览撰写了所有的文字资料，并提供了所有的文物。

展览的线索，是通过精心挑选的"陶器、雕塑、陶俑和银币"文物来传达的。这些文物向我们讲述了普利亚大区与地中海之间的关系。地中海一直是各种文化的交汇点，在古代，普利亚大区的农业和海洋资源滋养了贾皮吉、梅萨皮、普乌西蒂、道尼和塔兰蒂尼的人民，让希腊人和罗马人之间建立了特别而深厚的关系，也让该地区的神话故事和宗教信仰得以蓬勃发展。展览突出展现了小麦和普利亚土地上其他作物的核心角色，葡萄和橄榄、音乐、舞蹈、剧院、工艺，以及普利亚故事中流行艺术的表现也在其中。普利亚大区的文化植根于希腊和罗马的神话与历史，并将在未来大放异彩。

The gifts of the Gods to Apulia yesterday and today

Professor of University of Bari, Italy
Giuliano Volpe

Apulia, an extreme offshoot of the Italian peninsula towards the East, surrounded by the sea for over 800 kilometers, located in the heart of the Mediterranean, has received many gifts from the Gods in ancient times. The Apulian territory, corresponding to the heel and the heel of the 'boot' of Italy, is a sort of long peninsula and is very articulated in terms of geography and landscape, with mountainous areas, wide plains, and Murgia territories, with a millennial overlapping of cultures and civilizations. Fertile land, wide plains and soft hills, suitable for cereal cultivation and the cultivation of wine and oil, ample pastures for horses, flocks of sheep, cattle, forest-covered heights, coastal lagoons, salt marshes, a sea full of fish and many other resources. We could call it Apulia Felix, because it is fertile, productive, bearing fruit.

This is why, in order to illustrate to the Chinese public some aspects of the ancient history of this region, we have decided to resort to some particularly significant divinities of the Greco-Roman pantheon to celebrate some peculiar Apulian productions, both past and present.

从昨天到今天，
众神给予普利亚的礼物

意大利巴里大学教授
朱利安诺·沃尔佩

Guiding visitors along the exhibition route and ideally on a journey through Apulia's history is the young man on a dolphin. The dolphins that still inhabit the waters of Taranto, the Greek city of the two seas literally nestled between the Ionian and Adriatic Seas, are in various ways linked to the mythical tale of the ancient maritime relationship between Greece and Apulia. According to mythical tradition, the hero Taras, son of the sea god Poseidon and the nymph Satyria and husband of Minos' daughter, is said to have spotted a dolphin while on the shores of Japigia performing sacrifices in honor of his father and to have founded a settlement here dedicated to his mother Satyria.

The Spartan settlers led by Phalanthos, founder of the colony in the 8th century BC, were given the name of the ancient hero Taras. Leaving Sparta after receiving an oracle at Delphi, as always obscure and not easy to interpret ("I grant you to inhabit Satyrion and the rich land of Taras and to be the ruin of the Japigi" and again, as a sign to recognize the place, "when you see clear rain from the sky, you will conquer territory and cities"), they would set out for the West, amidst stormy seas and a shipwreck, from which Phalanthos would be saved thanks to a dolphin. Having left without a precise destination, Phalanthus, exhausted by the journey and discouraged, fell asleep on the knees of his wife Etra (whose name means 'clear sky'), who was also

普利亚是意大利亚平宁半岛向东方延伸的最远分支，被超过800公里的海洋环绕，地处地中海中心，在古代受到了众神的许多恩赐。意大利版图如同一个女性高跟靴，普利亚就是"靴子"的后跟。地理位置优越，地面景观复杂。从森林覆盖的高地到柔软的山丘，再到广阔的平原，这里土地肥沃，绿意盎然，不仅适合种植小麦，也适合种植葡萄树、橄榄树。广阔的牧场，适合马匹、羊群、牛群，沿海潟湖、盐沼，有不同的鱼类和许多海洋生物，另外还有丰富的石油资源。这里称"丰饶的普利亚"，因为这里是肥沃、多产、硕果累累的地方。

为了向中国观众展示普利亚古代历史的特别之处，我们决定使用"希腊与罗马神殿"中一些特别重要的神灵来讲述普利亚的过去和现在。

进入展厅，骑着海豚的年轻人将带领参观者沿着展览路线前进，体验普利亚的历史之旅。塔兰托是希腊的两海之城，坐落于爱琴海和亚得里亚海之间，直到今天，仍然有栖息在塔兰托水域的海豚，以特别的方式，将希腊与普利亚之间关于古代海神的故事联系在一起。根据神话传说，英雄塔拉斯是海神波塞冬和仙女萨蒂里亚的儿子，也是米诺斯女儿的丈夫。根据传说，塔拉斯在塔兰托的雅皮吉亚海岸纪念他的父亲时发现了一只海豚，他认为这是一个特别的象征，于是在这里建立了城市，这也是他献给母亲萨蒂里亚的礼物。

公元前8世纪，希腊斯巴达的统治者法兰托斯到达这里，并决定使用古代英雄塔拉斯的名字来命名这个城市。某一天，他在希腊德尔菲接受神谕，神谕告诉他，"我允许你居住在萨特利翁和塔拉斯的富饶土地上，在晴朗的天空下，成为贾皮吉人的领导"，"当你看到天空晴雨时，你将征服领土和城市"，他对神的话不太理解，离开斯巴达后，他们向西方出发，在波涛汹涌的大海上，船只即将沉没，此时，海上出现了一只海豚，将法兰托斯拯救出来。由于没有明确的可去的地方，法兰图斯在旅途中疲惫不堪，灰心丧气，在妻子埃特拉（名字的意思是"晴朗的天空"）

distressed and began to cry: her tears caused Phalanthus to wake up, and in this episode he recognized that the oracle had come true.

Taranto was the only Greek colony in Apulia (while there were numerous Greek colonies in the territory of Magna Graecia and Sicily) precisely because the Apulian territory was occupied and controlled by powerful indigenous peoples, warriors, endowed with a rich economy and a solid social organization, the result of highly evolved civilizations: the Dauni in the north, the Peucetii in the center and the Messapi in the south.

The image of the dolphin carrying a young man, also linked to the myth of Apollo, God of the sanctuary of Delphi in Greece where Phalanthos had received the oracle before embarking on his colonial expedition, thus became a symbol of the city of Taranto through its coins.

This is why we have chosen coins to accompany each section of the exhibition, each time highlighting how the attributes of the young man on the dolphin and the symbols on the coins highlight various aspects of the productive and cultural history and resources of the

的膝盖上睡着了，埃特拉也很伤心，开始哭泣，她的眼泪把法兰托斯吵醒了。这个时刻，他理解了神的话，也知道神所说的是真的。

塔兰托是普利亚唯一的希腊殖民地（而在玛格纳和西西里岛境内有很多希腊殖民地），之所以没有被希腊殖民，是因为普利亚的土著人极其强大，从北部的道尼到中部的普乌西蒂，再到南部的梅萨皮城邦，这里经济发达，社会牢固，是当时文明程度最高的区域之一。

海豚身背年轻人的形象也与阿波罗神话有关，希腊德尔菲圣地的神法兰托斯在开始他的殖民探险之前，获得了关于海豚及塔拉斯的神谕，从银币上，我们可以看到塔兰托市的象征。

Greek city and the entire region.

The exhibition aims to illustrate, through a significant selection of objects - mainly figurative ceramics, sculptures, paintings, terracotta and gold smithery - but also through reconstructions, multimedia videos, images and drawings, some features of ancient Apulia, a region which, thanks to its Mediterranean centrality, has always been a place where cultures converged and whose agricultural and marine resources fed the tables in ancient times and were clothed in beliefs and tales also linked to the profound presence in the region first of the Greeks and then of the Romans.

Grain and other products of the earth, including above all vines and olives, are at the center of tales whose protagonists are the ancient gods also worshipped in this

这就是为什么我们选择硬币作为展览每一部分开始的原因。每一次的展示都能突出海豚骑手以及钱币上的标志对希腊城市及整个大区发展和文化历史及渊源方方面面的展现。

展览通过大量精选的展品——陶瓷、雕塑、绘画、赤土陶器，同时也通过多媒体视频、数码艺术作品、摄影图片来展示普利亚的一些特征。普利亚地区，由于处在地中海中心，一直是文化交汇的地方，其农业和海洋资源在古代为人们提供食物，以信仰和故事为背景，对希腊人及后期的罗马人影响深刻。

谷物和其他农业产品，尤其是葡萄树和橄榄，是此次展览叙述的核心，这些物品与普利亚地区古代的神灵崇拜，包括音乐、舞蹈和其他艺术的形成有着密切的联系，是普利亚大区过去数世纪乃至现在仍然具有的特征元素。

历史的发展跨越了几个世纪，从公元前 7 世纪到罗马时代末期（公元 5 世纪），普利亚的道尼亚、普乌西蒂亚和梅萨皮亚等当地城堡文明，与塔兰托希腊殖民地、新地

region, of which music, dance and other forms of the arts were (and still are) characteristic elements over the centuries.

The historical development spans several centuries, at least between the 7th-6th centuries B.C. and the end of the Roman Age (5th century A.D.), in the relationship between the indigenous civilizations of Daunia, Peucetia and Messapia, the Greek colony of Taranto and the arrival and affirmation of the new Mediterranean power of Rome.

The god of the sea Poseidon will lead us to the discovery of its resources, fish, but not only, mussels, purple sea snail, and even salt, a precious resource to which the hero Heracles was also linked, necessary in ancient times to preserve food, fundamental in human and animal nutrition, in medicine and cosmetics, and in the treatment of skins and wool. Even today, Apulia is closely linked to the resources of the sea, to fishing, and even in its cuisine the products of the sea are a constant presence.

Demeter is the very symbol of abundance, fertility, the cycle of life. Linked to her is the image of wheat and various other cereals. In ancient, mediaeval and modern times, Apulia was and still is one of the great granaries of Italy and its bread is celebrated throughout the world, even with products that have won high honors, such as the bread of Altamura or that of Monte Sant'Angelo.

Athena, warrior goddess, beautiful, strong and intelligent, is at the origin of the birth of the olive tree: Apulia, with its centuries-old olive trees, true works of art of nature, and with one of the world's main oil productions, still seems to pay homage to Athena.

In Apulia, the cult of Athena is closely linked to the events, between history and myth, of the Trojan War and the founding of Rome: recently in Castro, a pretty town in the Salento region, archaeological excavations led to the discovery of a large temple of Athena and the discovery of

中海强国罗马之间，有着紧密的关系。

海神波塞冬将带领我们发现它的宝藏、鱼类、贻贝、紫色的海螺……还有英雄赫拉克勒斯所代表的盐，也是我们的宝贵资源，使用盐，保存并烹饪食物，让人类与动物获得营养。盐也是医药、化妆品、皮革和羊毛处理的基础。时至今日，普利亚与海洋资源、海洋渔业息息相关，甚至出名的普利亚美食中，海洋产品也是重要的一部分。

德墨忒耳是富饶、生育力和生命循环的象征。与她关联的是小麦和各种谷物。从古至今，普利亚是意大利最大的粮仓之一，它的面包在全世界都享有盛誉，其中包括阿尔塔穆拉面包、蒙特桑特面包等获得了很高荣誉的产品。

雅典娜，美丽、坚强、聪明的战士女神，橄榄树的象征与起点——普利亚拥有众多的古老的橄榄树，是世界橄榄油的最大产地之一。绵延百里的橄榄树林，是天然的艺术作品，它们在大自然的田野中，向雅典娜致敬。

在普利亚，"雅典娜、特洛伊战争、罗马帝国建立……"历史与神话故事密切关联。最近在萨伦托地区的小镇卡斯特罗，考古发掘发现了一个大型雅典娜神庙和一座在本次展览中的雅典娜雕像。奥古斯都时代的伟大诗人维吉尔在《埃涅阿斯纪》第三卷中写道，普利亚就是埃涅阿斯在意大利的登陆点，东方与西方、特洛伊与罗马的兴衰之间因此建立了联系，罗马从此成为当时的世界强国。特洛伊在遭受城市毁灭之后，流放者们从小亚细亚的达尔达尼亚航行穿过地中海，到达尔达努斯的故乡拉提姆，从布特林特横渡亚得里亚海后，在普利亚登陆，在那里他们发现了雅典娜密涅瓦神庙。罗马在扩张的早期阶段，以雅典娜·伊利亚卡的名义与普利亚的土著建立了联盟，萨伦托地区对雅典娜的崇拜很普遍，卢切拉和卡诺萨的神庙就表明了这一点。事实上，荷马所颂扬的著名亚该亚英雄狄俄墨得斯，与奥德修斯一起毁灭了特洛伊，据说他从特洛伊雅典娜神庙里偷走了雅典娜神像，并战后来到普利亚，在亚得里亚海建立了城市。最重要的是，他带来了希腊文明，特别是关于航海的技术和养马的文化。

雅典娜，在拉丁语中被称为密涅瓦，她也是文化、科学、

a monumental cult statue, a copy of which is on display in the exhibition. Virgil, the great poet of the age of Augustus, in the third book of the Aeneid, points to this very spot as the landing point of Aeneas in Italy: a link is thus established between East and West, between the vicissitudes of Troy and those of Rome, destined to become a world power. The Trojan exiles, after suffering the destruction of their city, sailed across the Mediterranean from Dardania, in Asia Minor, to Dardanus' original homeland, Latium, and after crossing the Adriatic from Butrint they landed there where they spotted a temple of Athena-Minerva. In the name of Athena Iliaca, Rome established an alliance in the early stages of its expansion with the indigenous peoples of Apulia, where the cult of Athena was widespread, as the temples of Lucera and Canosa, for instance, show. In fact, the famous Achaean hero Diomedes, celebrated by Homer, protagonist with Odysseus of the destruction of Troy, is said to have stolen the Palladium from the temple of Athena in Troy and, after the war, came to Apulia and other places in the Adriatic, founding cities and, above all, bringing with him the Greek civilization and, in particular, the culture of navigation and horse breeding.

Athena, the Latin Minerva, was also the patron deity of culture, science, research, arts and crafts. In the same way, Apollo protected the arts and specifically music, as well as philosophical thought, medical science and prophetic abilities: Apulia, with its universities and research centers, publishing houses (just think of the Bari-based Laterza publishing house, linked to the name of Benedetto Croce and many other intellectuals) and many other cultural enterprises, the creativity of craftsmen, the genius of musicians and artists, the depth of thought and the capacity for innovation of researchers is one of the territories in which the legacy of the two deities is still very much alive today.

Apulia is also the land of the pleasures of life, of banqueting rituals and conviviality, it is a land of vineyards and excellent wines: the powerful reds such as Primitivo di Manduria, Primitivo di Gioia del Colle, Nero di Troia, Negroamaro, Salice Salentino, Susumaniello, Castel del Monte, Cacc'e Mmitte di Lucera, San Severo, the very pleasant rosés, in which the region excels, the fresh whites such as Locorotondo, Martina, Verdeca, Bombino, the sweet Muscat wines, and many more. Dionysus is at home here.

Wine production has an ancient tradition and for centuries in Roman times wine was exported all over the Mediterranean in amphorae produced in the Brindisi area. We have chosen a precious dining room, from a Roman villa (Faragola, in the countryside of Ascoli Satriano), a farm owned by a rich and cultured member of the Roman aristocracy, to document the long persistence of the Dionysian world, of the civilization of banqueting, of the care of the body and the pleasures of life, even in the final stages of Antiquity, in the 5th century AD, when the Christian religion replaced the pagan one.

Finally, Heracles, the most popular of heroes, famous for his superhuman strength, armed with his unfailing club and covered in a lion's skin, a god and yet a man, with all his weaknesses, sufferings and even his mistakes, always capable of getting back up and facing a new hardship. In Roman times he also took on the role of protector of sheep farming and of the sheep-tracks of the transhumance, the great grassy roads that are still present in the Apulian landscape today, along which the seasonal movement of the flocks of sheep between the winter pastures on the Apulian plains and the summer pastures in the mountains of central Italy took place. Heracles was also linked to the supply of

研究、艺术和手工艺的守护神。同样，阿波罗也保护艺术，他是音乐、哲学思想、医学和预言能力的保护神。普利亚拥有大学研究中心和出版社（位于巴里的拉泰尔扎出版社，该出版社与贝内代托·克罗齐和许多其他知识分子的名字有关）。如今，普利亚还有很多富有创造力的文化企业，他们的工匠的创造力、音乐和艺术的天分，企业研发人员的深度思想和创新能力，仍然体现着雅典娜与阿波罗的思想精髓，也能感受神话遗产，至今仍然非常活跃而有效。

普利亚也是充满生活乐趣、宴会众多的欢乐之地，这是一片葡萄园和佳酿之地。普利亚出产的红葡萄酒、醇厚而强劲，如曼杜里亚普里米蒂沃葡萄酒、焦亚德尔科莱普里米蒂沃葡萄酒、黑托雅葡萄酒、黑曼罗葡萄酒、萨利切萨伦蒂诺葡萄酒、苏曼尼洛葡萄酒、蒙特城堡葡萄酒、卢切拉的卡克·米特葡萄酒（Cacc'e Mmitte di Lucer）、圣塞韦罗葡萄酒……普利亚也出产温和迷人的玫瑰粉色葡萄酒、温润浪漫的白葡萄酒，例如洛克罗通多葡萄酒、马丁娜葡萄酒、维黛卡葡萄酒、博比诺葡萄酒，还有甜美的麝香葡萄酒等。如此多的美酒，若酒神狄俄尼索斯在这里，他将感觉如同在家里一样。

葡萄酒酿制是普利亚的传统。在罗马时代，葡萄酒通过布林迪西地区生产的双耳细颈陶瓶出口到整个地中海。为了还原历史、还原酒神狄俄尼索斯文化、宴会文明及身体护理和生活乐趣的场景，我们选择了一栋罗马别墅（位于法拉戈拉，在阿斯科利萨特里亚诺的乡村地带）中的客厅，这里曾经是罗马贵族的农场，即使是在古罗马时代的末期，公元5世纪基督教文化取代了异教的时候，酒神文化也仍然存在着。

最后是赫拉克勒斯，他是希腊神话中最受欢迎的大力英雄。他披着狮皮，手里拿着棍棒，以超人的力量而闻名。他既是神又是人，像人一样有弱点，会犯错误，也会感受到痛苦，但他总是能够重新振作起来，勇敢面对新的困难。在罗马时代，他还是畜牧业和农场的保护神，在今天的普利亚，我们仍然可以看到羊群季节性地迁徙。冬天，大量

salt, a precious commodity for the animals. Even today, the large salt pans of Margherita di Savoia are a peculiarity of the Apulian landscape. Finally, Heracles was honored in ancient times by the Mercator's, the merchants, whose courage and vitality still represent a dowry of the Apulian merchant class.

This is a brief summary of the meaning of this exhibition, aimed at the Chinese people, heirs to a great cultural tradition, who share with Italy and Apulia many peculiarities that we have tried to indicate through gods and heroes: the work ethic and the commitment to produce abundance and wealth for all, the courage and ability to face new challenges, the relationship with nature, the sea, the countryside, the civilization of food, the cult for the quality of products, the pleasure of conviviality, the love for culture, the arts, creativity, the sense of hospitality, the strong bond with their own traditions, their history, their roots and, at the same time, the openness and interest in other cultures. We hope, therefore, that the exhibition, with the journey we propose in the company of gods and heroes, will stimulate visitors' curiosity and desire to travel around Puglia to discover its cities, museums, archaeological parks, traditions and cultures, and the many histories stratified in its landscapes.

的羊群到达普利亚的平原，夏日，它们重返意大利中部的高山牧场。赫拉克勒斯还与盐的生产有关，盐是所有动物包括人类生活的必需品。普利亚盛产盐，直至今日，位于萨沃亚玛格丽塔的大盐田仍然是普利亚景观的一大亮点。最后，赫拉克勒斯是古代贸易与商人的保护神，他的勇气，不畏困难的活力与韧性，今天仍旧被普利亚的商业贸易界所推崇。

这是展览的简要概括，写给中国的观众。与意大利和普利亚一样，中国拥有悠久辉煌的历史，你们也是中国文化传统的传承者。在这里，通过希腊的神话故事，我要告诉大家：所有人都应该有面对挑战的勇气和解决问题的能力，为社会创造财富的承诺与职责。懂得处理与自然、海洋、乡村的关系，尊重并倡导自然的食物，并创造高品质的食物。寻求艺术、文化、各类创造力所带来的快乐，懂得自己传统历史的根源，并对其他外来文化保持开放的态度和兴趣。因此，我们希望这次由众神陪伴的展览旅程可以激发观众的好奇心，让观众想要前往普利亚旅行，探索这里的城市、博物馆、考古公园、以及精彩的传统和文化，在自然风景中寻找其他历史痕迹。

致 谢
Acknowledgements

意大利普利亚荣誉委员会
COMITATO D'ONORE REGIONE PUGLIA

普利亚大区主席｜米歇尔·埃米利亚诺

Presidenza Regione Puglia ｜ MICHELE EMILIANO

意大利文化部博物馆总干事｜马西莫·奥桑娜

Direzione Generale Musei – Ministero della Cultura ｜ MASSIMO OSANNA

意大利文化部考古美术及景观司司长｜路易吉·拉罗卡

Direzione Generale Archeologia Belle Arti e Paesaggio – Ministero della Cultura ｜ LUIGI LA ROCCA

意大利巴里大学校长｜斯特凡诺·布伦兹尼

Università degli Studi di Bari "Aldo Moro" ｜ STEFANO BRONZINI

意大利福贾大学校长｜洛伦佐·洛穆齐奥

Università degli Studi di Foggia ｜ LORENZO LO MUZIO

意大利萨兰托大学校长｜法比奥·波利斯

Università del Salento ｜ FABIO POLLICE

意大利普利亚大区文化总监暨普利亚地区理事会成员｜格拉齐亚·迪巴瑞

Consigliera Delegata per la Cultura Regione Puglia ｜ GRAZIA DI BARI

执行人
PROPONENT

普利亚大区文化旅游与领土部部长｜阿尔多·帕特鲁诺

Direttore Dipartimento Turismo, Economia della Cultura e Valorizzazione del Territorio Regione Puglia ｜ ALDO PATRUNO

项目合作伙伴
PARTNER DI PROGETTO

普利亚博物馆地区管理局

DIREZIONE REGIONALE MUSEI PUGLIA

普利亚文化部地区秘书处

SEGRETARIATO REGIONALE DEL MINISTERO DELLA CULTURA PER LA PUGLIA

塔兰托国家考古博物馆

MARTA - MUSEO ARCHEOLOGICO NAZIONALE DI TARANTO

国家水下文化遗产监管局

SOPRINTENDENZA NAZIONALE PER IL PATRIMONIO CULTURALE SUBACQUEO

巴里市考古、美术和景观监管局

SOPRINTENDENZA ARCHEOLOGIA BELLE ARTI E PAESAGGIO PER LA CITTÀ METROPOLITANA DI BARI

巴莱塔 — 安德里亚 — 特拉尼省和福贾省考古、美术和景观监管局

SOPRINTENDENZA ARCHEOLOGIA BELLE ARTI E PAESAGGIO PER LE PROVINCE DI BARLETTA-ANDRIA-TRANI E FOGGIA

布林迪西省和莱切省考古、美术和景观监管局

SOPRINTENDENZA ARCHEOLOGIA BELLE ARTI E PAESAGGIO PER LE PROVINCE DI BRINDISI E LECCE

萨兰托大学文化遗产系

DIPARTIMENTO DI BENI CULTURALI UNIVERSITÀ DEL SALENTO

巴里大学人文研究与创新系

DIPARTIMENTO DI RICERCA E INNOVAZIONE UMANISTICA UNIVERSITÀ DEGLI STUDI DI BARI "ALDO MORO"

福贾大学人文、文学、文化遗产、教育科学系

DIPARTIMENTO DI STUDI UMANISTICI, LETTERE, BENI CULTURALI, SCIENZE DELLA FORMAZIONE, UNIVERSITÀ DEGLI STUDI DI FOGGIA

布林迪西图书馆博物馆中心

POLO BIBLIO-MUSEALI DI BRINDISI

福贾图书馆博物馆中心

POLO BIBLIOMUSEALE DI FOGGIA

莱切图书馆博物馆中心

POLO BIBLIOMUSEALE DI LECCE

普利亚公共剧院 — 地区艺术和文化联盟主席

TEATRO PUBBLICO PUGLIESE - CONSORZIO REGIONALE PER LE ARTI E LA CULTURA

意大利学术专家团队
SCIENTIFIC COMMITTE

1. 学术主任、意大利巴里大学教授｜朱利安诺·沃尔佩

Università degli Studi di Bari "Aldo Moro" ｜ Giuliano VOLPE (coordinatore),

2. 巴里市考古、美术和景观总监｜卡特琳娜·安内塞

Soprintendenza Archeologia Belle Arti e Paesaggio per la Città Metropolitana di Bari ｜ Caterina ANNESE

3. 巴里市考古、美术和景观总监｜琪琳娜·卡库迪

Soprintendente Archeologia Belle Arti e Paesaggio per la Città Metropolitana di Bari ｜ Giovanna CACUDI

4. 萨兰托大学林塞学院｜弗朗切斯科·德安德里亚

Università del Salento, Accademia dei Lincei ｜ Francesco D'ANDRIA

5. 国家水下文化遗产总监｜巴巴拉·达维德

Soprintendente Nazionale per il Patrimonio Culturale Subacqueo ｜ Barbara DAVIDDE

6. 博洛尼亚市民博物馆馆长｜埃娃·德格林诺切蒂

Direttrice Musei Civici di Bologna ｜ Eva DEGL'INNOCENTI

7. 巴里市考古、美术和景观总监丨埃莱娜·德卢卡

Soprintendenza Archeologia Belle Arti e Paesaggio per la Città Metropolitana di Bari ｜ Elena DELLU'

8. 普利亚大区文化旅游与领土部丨路易吉·德卢卡

Dipartimento Turismo, Economia della Cultura e Valorizzazione del Territorio Regione Puglia ｜ Luigi DE LUCA

9. 福贾大学丨里卡多·迪切萨雷

Università degli Studi di Foggia ｜ Riccardo DI CESARE

10. 巴里大学丨朱塞佩娜·加达莱塔

Università degli Studi di Bari ｜ Giuseppina GADALETA

11. 巴莱塔 — 安德里亚 — 特拉尼省和福贾省考古、美术和景观总监丨安妮塔·瓜尼埃里

Soprintendente Archeologia Belle Arti e Paesaggio per le province di Barletta-Andria-Trani e Foggia ｜ Anita GUARNIERI

12. 国家研究中心文化遗产科学研究所丨托马索·伊斯梅利

Istituto di Scienze del Patrimonio Culturale–Centro Nazionale delle Ricerche, CNR ｜ Tommaso ISMAELLI

13. 福贾大学丨达尼洛·莱奥内

Università degli Studi di Foggia ｜ Danilo LEONE

14. 塔兰托国家考古博物馆馆长，普利亚博物馆地区管理局丨克劳迪娅·卢切塞

DirettricE MArTA, Direzione Regionale Musei Puglia ｜ Claudia LUCCHESE

15. 普利亚博物馆地区管理局丨弗朗切斯科·隆戈巴尔迪

Direzione Regionale Musei Puglia ｜ Francesco LONGOBARDI

16. 萨莱诺省和阿维利诺省考古、美术和景观总监丨洛伦佐·曼奇尼

Soprintendenza Archeologia Belle Arti e Paesaggio per le province di Salerno e Avellino ｜ Lorenzo MANCINI

17. 萨兰托大学丨卡蒂娅·曼尼诺

Università del Salento ｜ Katia MANNINO

18. 布林迪西图书馆博物馆中心丨艾米莉亚·曼诺齐

Polo Bibliomuseale di Brindisi ｜ Emilia MANNOZZI

19. 普利亚博物馆地区管理局丨劳拉·马西埃洛

Direzione Regionale Musei Puglia ｜ Luca MERCURI

20. 布林迪西省和莱切省考古、美术和景观总监丨朱塞佩·穆奇

Soprintendenza Archeologia Belle Arti e Paesaggio per le province di Brindisi e Lecce ｜ Giuseppe MUCI

21. 巴莱塔 — 安德里亚 — 特拉尼省和福贾省考古、美术和景观总监丨伊塔洛·玛丽亚·穆顿尼

Soprintendenza Archeologia Belle Arti e Paesaggio per le province di Barletta-andria-Trani e Foggia ｜ Italo Maria MUNTONI

22. 普利亚大区文化旅游与领土部部长丨阿尔多·帕特鲁诺

Direttore Dipartimento Turismo, Economia della Cultura e Valorizzazione del Territorio Regione Puglia ｜ ALDO PATRUNO

23. 普利亚文化部地区秘书处丨玛丽亚·皮卡雷塔

Segretariato Regionale del Ministero della Cultura per la Puglia ｜ Maria PICCARRETA

24. 普利亚公共剧院 — 地区艺术和文化联盟丨保罗·庞齐奥

Teatro Pubblico Pugliese - Consorzio regionale per le Arti e la Cultura ｜ Paolo PONZIO

25. 布林迪西省和莱切省考古、美术和景观总监丨弗朗西斯卡·里奇奥

Soprintendente Archeologia Belle Arti e Paesaggio per le province di Brindisi e Lecce ｜ Francesca RICCIO

26. 布林迪西省和莱切省考古、美术和景观总监丨塞雷娜·斯特拉费拉

Soprintendenza Archeologia Belle Arti e Paesaggio per le province di Brindisi e Lecce ｜ Serena STRAFELLA

27. 普利亚大区文化旅游与领土部（主策展人） ｜ 安娜·露西娅·坦佩斯塔

Dipartimento Turismo, Economia della Cultura e Valorizzazione del Territorio Regione Puglia (coordinamento) ｜ Anna Lucia TEMPESTA

展品提供
PLENDERS

玛塔 — 塔兰托国家考古博物馆

MARTA - MUSEO ARCHEOLOGICO NAZIONALE DI TARANTO

西吉斯蒙多 — 卡斯特罗梅迪亚诺博物馆

MUSEO SIGISMONDO CASTROMEDIANO DI LECCE

卡诺萨国家考古博物馆

MUSEO ARCHEOLOGICO NAZIONALE DI CANOSA

恩格纳西亚国家考古博物馆

MUSEO ARCHEOLOGICO NAZIONALE DI EGNAZIA

雅达博物馆

MUSEO NAZIONALE JATTA DI RUVO DI PUGLIA

阿尔塔穆拉博物馆

MUSEO ARCHEOLOGICO NAZIONALE DI ALTAMURA

里贝佐布林迪西博物馆

MUSEO RIBEZZO DI BRINDISI

福贾市民博物馆

MUSEO CIVICO DI FOGGIA

普利亚博物馆地区管理局

DIREZIONE REGIONALE MUSEI PUGLIA

巴里市考古、美术和景观监管局

SOPRINTENDENZA ARCHEOLOGIA BELLE ARTI E PAESAGGIO PER LA CITTÀ METROPOLITANA DI BARI

巴莱塔 — 安德里亚 — 特拉尼省和福贾省考古、美术和景观总局

SOPRINTENDENZA ARCHEOLOGIA BELLE ARTI E PAESAGGIO PER LE PROVINCE DI BARLETTA-ANDRIA-TRANI E FOGGIA

布林迪西省和莱切省考古、美术和景观总局

SOPRINTENDENZA ARCHEOLOGIA BELLE ARTI E PAESAGGIO PER LE PROVINCE DI BRINDISI E LECCE

国家水下文化遗产监管局

SOPRINTENDENZA NAZIONALE PER IL PATRIMONIO CULTURALE SUBACQUEO

曼弗雷多尼亚国家考古博物馆

MUSEO ARCHEOLOGICO NAZIONALE DI MANFREDONIA

意大利提供文字英文编辑
ENGLISH EDITING OF TEXT PROVIDED BY LTALIAN TEAM

总撰稿｜朱利安诺·沃尔佩 / 安娜·露西亚·坦佩斯塔

edited by：Giuliano VOLPE / Anna Lucia TEMPESTA

文字撰写｜

朱利安诺·沃尔佩 / 卡特琳娜·安内塞 / 弗朗切斯科·德安德里亚 / 埃莱娜·德卢卡 / 里卡多·迪切萨雷 / 文森扎．迪斯塔西 / 朱塞佩娜·加达莱塔 /

托马索·伊斯梅利 / 达尼洛·莱奥内 / 克劳迪娅·卢切塞 / 洛伦佐·洛穆齐奥 / 卡蒂娅·曼尼诺 / 阿尔多·帕特鲁诺 / 安娜·露西亚·坦佩斯塔

Test｜

Giuliano VOLPE/ Caterina ANNESE / Francesco D'ANDRIA / Elena DELLU'/ Riccardo DI CESARE / Vincenza DISTASI / Giuseppina GADALETA/

Tommaso ISMAELLI / Danilo LEONE / Claudia LUCCHESE / Lorenzo MANCINI/ Katia MANNINO / Aldo PATRUNO / Anna Lucia TEMPESTA

图片版权归属
IMAGE COPYRIGHT

Fotografie，Le immagini sono tratte da

普利亚之光，作者｜米莫·阿塔代莫

PUGLIA IN LUCE ，diMimmo Attademo

普利亚大区委员会，《阅读普利亚》刊物， 2022 年第 99 册， 巴里编辑版本

Consiglio Regionale della Puglia, *Leggi la Puglia* Pubblicazione No. 99 della linea editoriale, Repertori, Quorum Edizioni, Bari 2022

"双海—新一代旅游发展项目"-2014 / 2020 年 IPA CBC 意大利 - 阿尔巴尼亚 - 黑山文化自主项目

"DUE MARI" Next Generation Tourism Development – Project financed by Programme Interreg IPA CBC Italy-Albania-Montenegro 2014/2020

意大利文化部 — 普利亚地区博物馆管理局

Ministero della Cultura Italia - Direzione regionale Musei Puglia

意大利文化部 — 巴里市考古、美术和景观监管局 / 塔兰托国家考古博物馆

Ministero della Cultura - Direzione SABAP / MARTA

图片拍摄
PHOTOGRAGHY

米莫·阿塔代莫 / 万达·比法尼 / 加埃塔诺·焦尔达诺 / 米莫＆贾科莫·古利埃尔米 / 乔尼安 / 安德烈·皮斯托莱西 / 拉法埃莱·普斯 /

罗伯托·罗卡 / 瓦伦蒂诺·罗曼诺 / 卡洛斯·索丽都 / 安东尼奥＆罗伯托·塔塔格里昂 / 安吉洛·突迪斯

Mimmo ATTADEMO / Vanda BIFFANI / Gaetano GIORDANO/ Mimmo & Giacomo GUGLIELMI / JONIAN / Andrea PISTOLESI / Raffaele PUCE / Roberto ROCCA /

A. Valentino ROMANO / Carlos SOLITO / Antonio & Roberto TARTAGLIONE / Angelo TUNDIS

We met and parted with the exhibition at the Oriental Metropolitan Museum (the 3rd-6th century) from the height of summer to late fall. Just as the slogan of the exhibition said, this is a spiritual journey across the East and West, through the ancient and modern. This exhibition can be said to be the eternal splendor of my heart. On the day the exhibition ended, the Oriental Metropolitan Museum (the 3rd-6th century) put an exclamation mark on the exhibition in the form of a closing sharing session, which can also be said to be an ellipsis rather than a period. 120 days of the exhibition period, I think the splendor of the exhibition consists of the following parts:

The first splendor is the wonderful exhibit. Thanks to the joint efforts of our curatorial team, more than 110 wonderful exhibits from eight national museums and some archaeological institutions in Italy across the ocean are presented to the audience.

The second splendor is the team spirit of curation. The professors, experts and staff from Italy represented by Volpe and Anna, the leading comrades from ART EXHIBITIONS CHINA represented by Luo Lijun and Wang Yu, the team members from Plandi represented by Hong Quan, and the partners from the Oriental Metropolitan Museum (the 3rd-6th century) represented by Director Zhang Lei of the Department of Integrated Business. They collectively presented such a wonderful exhibition for us.

The third splendor is the splendor of volunteer service. Volunteer Mr. Luo Jian once said that this exhibition explanation was a blind-box explanation because none of the volunteers had ever seen the exhibits until it was carried out. Even so, the volunteers' explanation service during the exhibition period was still a wonderful and professional presentation. On the day of the exhibition ended, the young volunteers of the Oriental Metropolitan Museum took pictures in the exhibition hall and kept saying that it was the most wonderful exhibition they had ever seen.

后 记

南京市博物总馆副馆长
宋 燕

The fourth splendor is the highlight of external publicity. Many media worked together to publicize this exhibition, from the beginning to during the exhibition, until the last week of the exhibition, including many tweets written by the Oriental Metropolitan Museum (the 3rd-6th century) partners themselves. The online course of the Oriental Metropolitan Museum (the 3rd-6th century) was still being promoted until the last week, throughout the whole process. The external publicity of the exhibition was very bright and wonderful.

During the summer this year, the Oriental Metropolitan Museum (the 3rd-6th century) was the first in the national museum community to eliminate Monday closing hours, which generated a lot of attention. With the extended opening hours, more audiences were able to enjoy this cultural feast. The exhibition will soon go to the Guangzhou Maritime Museum. It is because so many museums have launched high-quality exhibitions one after another that museums have become an integral part of city life. It is through the relay of museums that a platform for civilization exchange and mutual understanding has been built. Let's feel the power of culture in the museums, and work together towards a better life and a better future.

从盛夏到深秋，展览在六朝博物馆与我们相遇，又与我们离别。正如展览宣传语所述，这是一场跨越东西、穿越古今的心灵之旅，这场展览可以说是我心中永恒的绚美。展览结束的当天，六朝博物馆用闭幕分享会的形式为展览画上了一个惊叹号，也可以说是省略号而不是句号。120天的展期，展览的精彩由以下几部分组成：

第一，是有精彩的展品。110 多件精彩的展品来自意大利的 8 个国家博物馆和一些考古机构，在我们策展团队的共同努力下，跨越重洋，展现在观众面前。

第二，是策展的团队精神。意大利方以沃尔佩、安娜为代表的教授专家和工作人员，中国文物交流中心以罗利君、王宇为代表的领导同志们，普兰迪公司以洪泉为代表的团队成员们，还有六朝博物馆以张蕾主任为代表的综合业务部的伙伴们，他们共同为我们呈现了这样一场精彩的展览。

第三，是志愿服务的精彩。志愿者罗建老师曾说这次展览讲解是一次开盲盒的讲解，因为直到开展前，志愿者们都没有见过展品。即便是这样，在展期内志愿者们的讲解服务仍然是专业地呈现。展览结束当天，六朝博物馆的志愿者们在展厅中留影，还一直在说这是自己看到的最精彩的展览。

第四，是对外宣传的精彩。多家媒体共同为这个展览做宣传，从开展前到开展中，直到展览结束的最后一个星期都在做宣推，包括六朝博物馆编写的一篇篇推文。六朝博物馆的线上课程到最后一周还在推送，贯穿始终。展览的对外宣传非常精彩，非常有亮点。

2023 年暑假期间，六朝博物馆在全国博物馆界率先取消周一闭馆制度，引发了广泛关注。延长开放时间后，更多观众得以共飨这场文化盛宴。展览即将奔赴广州海事博物馆，正是因为有这么多博物馆一家接着一家推出高质量的展览，才让博物馆成为城市生活不可或缺的一部分。正是通过一家家博物馆的接力，才搭建起了一个文化交流互鉴的平台。让我们在博物馆感受文化的力量，共同迈向美好的生活、美好的未来。